Minnie Walter Myers

Romance and Realism of the Southern Gulf coast

Minnie Walter Myers

Romance and Realism of the Southern Gulf coast

ISBN/EAN: 9783337033590

Printed in Europe, USA, Canada, Australia, Japan

Cover: Foto ©Thomas Meinert / pixelio.de

More available books at **www.hansebooks.com**

ROMANCE AND REALISM OF THE SOUTHERN GULF COAST

BY

MINNIE WALTER MYERS

※

CINCINNATI

THE ROBERT CLARKE COMPANY

To My Father,

HARVEY W. WALTER,

AND MY BROTHERS,

FRANK, AVENT, AND JAMES WALTER.

With an exalted heroism that
forgot all consideration of self,
they faced the terrors of an
epidemic, and sacrificed themselves that others might live.

———

*"Greater love hath no man than this, that a man
lay down his life for his friends."*

PREFACE.

Acknowledgments are due for assistance received from Claiborne's "History of Mississippi;" Gayarre's "Romances of Louisiana History;" Alcée Fortier's "Louisiana Studies;" "The Sketch-book of New Orleans;" "In Acadia," by Margaret Avery Johnston; "Letters on the Gulf Coast," by R. A. Wilkinson; "New Orleans, the Place and the People," by Grace King; "Legends and Lyrics of the Gulf Coast," by Laura F. Hinsdale, and "Ethnological Reports."

The history of a country is incomplete without the preservation of its romances. Collecting, condensing and arranging the material for this little volume has been tedious but fascinating work. The author has endeavored to make each scene characteristic and progressive from the founding of Louisiana to the present time.   THE AUTHOR.

MEMPHIS, April, 1898.

CONTENTS.

ix

ILLUSTRATIONS.

xi

ROMANCE AND REALISM OF THE SOUTHERN GULF COAST.

CHAPTER I.

The great Sun Chiefs of the Natchez tribe greeted the first morning beams of their celestial brother with a prolonged howl, then waving their hands from east to west, they showed him his daily path.

They did not know, however, nor could their great medicine men foretell them, that the sun of Indian happiness and prosperity would also cross the great Father of Waters, and would set in western darkness never to rise again.

The Choctaw Indian, the stoic of the woods, boasted in the face of Tecumseh's embittered eloquence in 1811, that Choctaw hands had never been stained in the blood of the white man. To him they had thrown open their wigwams, and offered, with proverbial Indian hospitality, to divide their maize. The paleface accepted the half, and then seized the fields upon which it grew. In the beginning,

such was the European gentleman and the untutored savage.

Even as Romulus and Remus were nurtured
by a wolf, so were the infant ancestors of the
Choctaws nurtured by a panther.   When they
were large enough to go into the woods the
great book-maker gave them their bows and
arrows and an earthen pot, and said to them,
" I give you these hunting grounds for your
homes.   When you leave them you die."

He then disappeared in the woods.   But
now, where are they?   The answer comes back
to us in the lament of the Choctaw chief ; its
beauty can never be marred, though it has been
so often repeated.

" Brother, when you were young we were
strong.   We fought by your side, but our arms
are now broken.   You have grown large ; my
people have become small.   My voice is weak.
It is not the voice of a warrior, but the wail of
an infant ; I have lost it in mourning over the
misfortunes of my people.   These are their
graves, and in these aged pines you hear the
ghosts of the departed.   Twelve winters ago
our chief sold our country.   If the dead had
been counted it would never have been made ;
but, alas! though they stood around they could
not be seen and heard.   Their tears come in

the rain-drops, and their voice in the wailing wind. When you took our country you promised us land. Twelve times have the trees dropped their leaves, and yet we have received no land. Is this *truth?* Grief has made children of us ; my people are small ; their shadow scarcely reaches to your knee ; they are scattered and gone."

No scholarly address could have furnished more profound eloquence. No rules of rhetoric were needed to improve the imagery of the red man. As the child of nature he drew his pictures directly from her heart.

The white man talks learnedly of an eclipse of the sun, and explains the scientific reasons for it. The Indians knew, however, that these dark disks upon its surface meant that black squirrels were attacking it to devour it. With wild alarm the whole tribe beat their drums and kettles, screamed, shot their arrows at the sun, and made every possible noise to frighten the squirrels. Surely they must have been squirrels, for after a short or prolonged warfare they disappeared, and the sun shone again with all his brilliance. These same noises frightened away the evil spirits of the dead.

The tallest tree fell beneath the touch of the

white man, but the Indian could tell of his ancient mammoth kindred, who devoured every thing, and, breaking down the forests, made the Mississippi prairies. A terrible earthquake had killed all but one. Affrighted, he had fled at one mighty leap across the Mississippi at Memphis and sought refuge in the Rocky Mountains.

At a time of great drought the elk and buffalo also fled across the Mississippi river, but the Biloxi Indian could tell you that the buffalo would forever carry with him the evidence of his defeat by their great Ancient of Frogs. This Ancient of Frogs was endowed by his grandmother with wonderful strength. The first antagonist he met was a panther, but the frog threw him against a tree and broke his jaw; then he encountered a bear, but throwing him against a tree he broke off his tail, which has accounted ever since for the short tail of the bear on the southern shore. When he met the buffalo he threw him against a tree and broke the buffalo's back, and to this day the latter bears a hump in evidence of his defeat. The last conflict was with a deer, whose leg was broken, but the Ancient of Frogs formed a great friendship for the deer. Now when we hear the shrill "pes! pes!" of the frogs, mingled with the

of the Southern Gulf Coast.

Martha Washington oak.

sounds of the splashing waves and sighing pines, we know that he is giving warning of danger to the deer and telling him that the hunters are near.

The Biloxi Indians never allowed a child to step over a grindstone, knowing that it would stop his growth. How clearly interwoven are the superstitions of different nations! The writer well remembers as a child that her dear old black mammy would say to her:

"Chile, don' yer neber lay down on de flo, an let nobody step ober yer, kase ef yer do yer won't neber gro' no mo."

The history of Natchez and Biloxi is so closely connected that it is almost a link within a link. The Natchez tribe did not dwell so directly upon the coast as the Biloxis, Pascagoulas, Choctaws and others, but they felt that it belonged equally to them. It was their frequent camping ground. There grew the giant oaks a thousand years old, whose roots striking deep into the earth found what Ponce de Leon sought in vain—the fountain of youth. Each spring they budded forth in their vernal freshness of beauty; the southern nightingale, the mocking bird, sang amongst their branches, and the long gray moss hung from each limb and stirred gently with every breeze. The

Indian loved the fragrant orange and magnolia trees, the soft balmy air, the palmettos uplifting their dagger-shaped leaves, the tall trembing reeds, the soft murmur of the pines, the stately cypress, and the ever-restless but musical sounds of the sea.

Some writers describe the Natchez as equaling the Montezumas in splendor; but their wigwams were rude and rough, and even their temple of the sun was only an oven-baked structure. It had simply a rough altar, and shelves around the wall with baskets containing the bones of the Great Suns; on lower shelves there were baskets containing the bones of favorite attendants, who had been killed to attend them to the Happy Hunting Grounds. Outside there was a fence of sharp pickets, and upon the point of each was the skull of an enemy.

When a warrior entered the hut of the Great Sun, the latter would be seated upon his bed of rude mats, and there was a stone in the middle of the room. The warrior howled when he entered, and before saluting the Great Sun he would run around the stone in the middle of the room three times, howling each time; the more he howled the greater the favor that would be extended to him. If he were of small importance the Great Sun noticed him only with a slight grunt; if more in favor the grunt would be more pronounced, but the warrior could never answer him without first howling.

When we study the customs and traditions of other people we are apt to receive many of them with a quiet smile of ridicule; but we should pause when we consider some of our own beliefs and matters of etiquette. The impression that we receive of a picture depends greatly upon the light in which it is viewed.

Mississippi was the first state in the Union to enact a law giving to woman the control of her own property; now it has emancipated her from all disabilities of coverture; but few persons know that the original statute was suggested by the tribal customs of the Chickasaw Indians in the northern part of the state. The despised squaw, who bore the heat and burden of the day, reached forth her small brown hands and struck off the shackles that bound her more civilized sister. Under the Chickasaw law the husband acquired no right to the property of the wife which she owned at the time of her marriage, or to the subsequent acquests, and no part was subject to the debts of her husband. The marriage ties were often lightly made and lightly broken; there were no divorce suits; but when husband and wife agreed to separate, the children belonged to the mother. Her rights were acknowledged supreme.

Many of the Indian laws were very just. When the husband and wife died leaving no children, the wife's relatives generally took the property, unless the husband had built the house entirely, when his relatives inherited it. Nothing could be fairer, for the Indian woman generally did all the work and built the home. Her life was one of absolute drudgery; but her burdens were laid upon a perfectly healthy body, one of God's greatest blessings, that does not generally come through doors closed to the fresh air of heaven and to bodies enervated by luxury. In those days there were in the forest no sanitariums filled with delicate women. The realistic thought will obtrude itself, that, if the white man has taken the burdens from the back of woman, he has sometimes, with refined cruelty, inflicted burdens upon her aching heart that are too heavy for her endurance.

Without any woman's suffrage movement, but in the quietest way, the Choctaw girl possessed in matters of courtship rights that are not granted to the Nineteenth Century girl.

The latter must wait in modest silence until she is wooed and won, though her heart should flutter like a bird and her cheeks crimson when she hears the footstep of her beloved. To the Indian girl belonged the privilege of giving the "first banter." This was done generally by squeezing the hand of her brave or by stepping upon his foot. Should he presume to give the first banter, she and all the squaws could fall upon him and beat him most unmercifully. In the majority of tribes the Indian could marry the sister of his dead wife. The peace of the tribe was not annually disturbed by the ghost of a deceased-wife's-sister bill.

The students of Yale and Harvard find no greater pleasure in the game of football than the red men of the southern shore. Particularly did they delight in the intricate game of ball played with a crooked stick, and they were fully equal to the present progressive age in the excitement and extent of their betting. An Indian runner could travel fifty miles a day, and when he brought war news he entered the village with a war-whoop. This was taken up by every one he met until he reached the town-house, in front of the public square. In health and symmetry of body the American Indian almost equaled the classic

Greek.   Disease and deformity were compara-
tively unknown among them.   Their system
of massage was as efficient as our own or that
of the Romans.

Around their blazing fires in the evening, or
in the soft summer moonlight, tradition told
them of their history, philosophy, religion and
customs.   To them the white man's "speaking
bark" was unknown ; tradition and sign language constituted their encyclopædia.   There
were so many tribes and dialects that in sign
language they were most proficient.

"Action is eloquence, and the eyes of the ignorant
More learned than their ears."

Their green corn dance was their annual
jubilee, when all wrongs except murder were
forgiven.   This was the season when fresh
fires were built, and the year started with new
happiness.   Nor shall we believe that their
dancing was irregular and unpracticed.   Their
intricate and regular steps equaled the drills of
our modern gymnasium, and with the dance was
mingled the sound of their joyous laughter and
rude but rhythmic music.   Nature smiled upon
her happy-hearted children.   The immense
live oaks, clad in their drapery of moss, lifted
their umbrageous arms above, shielding them

from sun and storm ; and the sea, catching the sounds of their revelry, held them in its depths, and gives them to us now in strange, mysterious music.

Nor did the heart of the Indian throb only with physical and material being. To him were given some of the fine instincts of right and wrong that would have done honor to the Virginia Cavalier or the New England Puritan. When they borrowed an article, they returned it promptly at the promised time. When condemned to death for murder, the Indian was free to go where he would until the day of execution, when he presented himself, made a mark around his heart for a target, and calmly met his doom. For him no officers of the law were needed.

They were keenly sensitive to ridicule and disgrace, and suicides among them for these causes were not unfrequent. Although they never mentioned their dead after burial, who knows what real bitter tears may have been mingled with their weird cry over the cold bodies, or what weight of bereavement and loss may have lingered in their hearts under a stolid exterior ? Nor do we know what vague thoughts they may have had of the Great Spirit—the Giver of Breath. The yearning to know the truth is universal.

The Natchez idea of heaven was a perpetual feast of green corn, venison and melons, and hades was to eat spoiled fish and alligators.

Even as the Sons and Daughters of the Revolution and all other patriots love their country, so did the Indian love his—before it was taken from him. The proudest boast of a Choctaw was, " I am a Choctaw." They loved not only their country, but also their homes and children ; and they loved their wives, however much they may have abused them—a characteristic sometimes observed in civilized as well as savage life. It is said the Pascagoula Indians, who dwelt in Southern Mississippi on the banks of the Escatawpa, loved its shores so dearly that nowhere else would they consent to be buried. When called away, either in the chase or upon the war-path, they first stooped and drank of the flowing Escatawpa, for there was some charm in its waters that always brought back the wanderer. Even now it is said :

> " He who drinks of Escatawpa's tide
> His bones must rest on Escatawpa's side."

Time was marked by bundles of sticks, one stick being withdrawn for each day. In this connection is told one of the sweetest stories of Fort Rosalie, now Natchez. The Natchez and Chickasaws had agreed to attack and surprise the fort at a certain time ; but Stellona, a princess of the royal blood, precipitated the attack of the Natchez before the Chickasaws came by extracting two arrows from the bundle. This she did to save the life of her French lover, Lieutenant De Mace.

There is scarcely a place in this charmed region of the South which does not have its romance. Even now, when the halcyon birds are flying in Indian summer, a soft gray haze is seen on the coast. This is said to be the smoke from the mysterious furnaces of the God of Pottery, who taught the Indians their knowledge of it, and who lingers here reluctant to leave these shores.

One of the most charming characteristics of nearly all Indian tribes was their hospitality. They regarded it more of a duty than a virtue. They considered that the Great Spirit gave the land equally to all, and that it was their duty to entertain the stranger and the needy—the first because he was away from home, and the latter because the land belonged equally to him. In the majority of Indian tribes, there were no stated hours for meals, but the pot was always kept boiling for the benefit of any

who might come hungry. Even the most
worthless of the tribe was never denied food;
but a lazy man who begged was so covered
with ridicule that an Indian tramp was rarely
seen. In this respect the American tramp is
far ahead of the Indian. Buckets of ridicule
may be poured over him without injury to his
feelings, if the ridicule is only intermixed with
a few cold biscuits and cups of coffee.

A number of Indian families generally lived
together, sharing things in common. At present the communistic feeling is growing in the
United States. Carried to an extreme, and in
the hands of ignorant and lawless classes, this
may lead us to grave evils, but it lends an interest to this Indian custom. Ethnologists call
our attention to the custom as tending to the
final equalization of subsistence. They assert
that hunger and destitution could not prevail
in one end of a village while plenty prevailed
in the other end of it.

In this chapter the habits of the Choctaw
Indians have especially been considered because they were the friends of the early colonists. The writer is indebted to Claiborne's
History of Mississippi for much interesting information.

Chactas and Chicks-a, two brothers, came

from the west led by a pole held by invisible hands. The pole stopped when it crossed the river and reached Mississippi soil. Chicks-a went to the northern part of Mississippi, and his tribe of Chickasaws became followers of the Red Cross of St. George ; while Chactas founded the Choctaw tribe in Southern Mississippi and Alabama, and they followed the Lily of France. Thus the foreigners brought with them to this country their seeds of envy and discord, and planted them in the hearts of the red men.

Perhaps it may be claimed that these pages have idealized the character of the Indian, and the character of the pale face has been depreciated. The terrible war-whoop, and the glittering tomahawk are shudderingly remembered ; but, turning the light of truth upon civilized history, we read of the Salem witchcraft, with its horrors, the Spanish Inquisition, the persecution of the Christian and the Jew, and the tyranny of unbounded power in every age. Realizing all this, and realizing that we have taken from the Indian his home and nearly exterminated his people, we should at least bury him with a requiem of justice.

CHAPTER II.

The humming bird foretold to the Biloxi Indians the arrival of strangers; it was also to them the bird of truth.

What myriads of them must have fluttered their brilliant wings in the sunlight on that fateful morning, in 1699, when the Indian discovered the great black birds with white wings, skimming slowly and gracefully the blue waters of their bay. Silently and swiftly the little birds of truth flew above them, trying in vain to tell the red men how freighted with change this scene was to them. Trying in vain to tell them that these strange creatures came from the old to the new world to change its customs, its people, and the very aspect of nature.

How strange it was to them when the royal looking Iberville and his younger, but not less noble-looking brother, Bienville, stepped upon the shore in their gorgeous dress, and with their retinue knelt beneath the golden cross, and took possession of the country in the name of their God and their king. More startling still

was the cannon's voice from its cloud of smoke
as it went thundering over the waters.

To the Biloxians their Thunder Being was
so strange and mysterious that his name was
never mentioned in cloudy weather. Fearful
were they that he would hear them, and in his
wrath frown down upon them in clouds of rain
and storm. It was only when he was far away
and the sun was shining, that they told, in awe-
struck tones, the stories of his power. Yet
these strange pale faces brought their thunder
with them, and, though the sun was shining, it
spoke or remained silent at their command.

These were not, however, the first white
men to step upon Mississippi soil. With his
brilliant but ill-fated cortege, with his Anda-
lusian steeds, his high hopes and bitter disappointments, Hernando de Soto had swept
from Florida to the banks of the Father of
Waters, which he first discovered just below
the site of the present city of Memphis in
May, 1541. He did not realize that this
mighty river, which was to be the source of
wealth and prosperity to so many others,
would be to him the sepulcher of his hopes,
his ambitions, and his body.

About one hundred and thirty years afterward, in 1673, Father Marquette and Joliet

A squaw and papoose.

came down from Quebec and sailed down its
waters as far as Arkansas. Being convinced
that it emptied into the gulf, they returned to
Quebec and reported their discovery amidst
the wildest rejoicings. In 1682, Cavelier de
la Salle was at the mouth of the Mississippi,
and took possession of it in the name of
France. When Iberville and Bienville landed
on the southern coast, the pulse of the country
from north to south was beginning to throb
with new and certain life; but while La Salle
had planned a French colony in the South,
Iberville and Bienville founded at Biloxi, in
1699, the first settlement of the great State of
Louisiana.

The sound is divided from the Gulf of
Mexico by a number of islands lying at vary-
ing distances from the shore. Between them
are channels and passes leading into the gulf.
Nearly all of these islands are low, sandy, and
unprepossessing, but there is not one that has
not its strange legends, and that has not been
connected with the history of the sea-coast.

Ship Island, the largest and most important,
was so named by the French because it was
the best roadstead for vessels. Its harbor has
always been remarkably safe against storms.
It has not only been a refuge for ships in time

of peace, but it has also been of greatest importance in time of war. During the war of 1812, Packenham's fleet was anchored in it; and during our late civil war, one of the first movements of the federal troops was the capture of Biloxi and Ship Island. During his reign in New Orleans, General Butler named the fort at Ship Island "Fort Massachusetts" in honor of his native state. In this fort he confined persons whom he desired to punish.

Cat Island was so named because when the French reached it, they found upon it a small animal, somewhat resembling both a fox and a cat. One of Iberville's men exclaimed, "This is the land of cats." This cat, however, was the American raccoon, which has since become so dear to the American darkies' heart and appetite that from it he has derived his sobriquet of "coons."

The American coon has borne his part in the history of the country, and is not to be ignored. In the memorable campaign of 1840, many wildly cheering processions of Whigs were headed by miniature log cabins with coons perched above them—the campaign of log cabins, coons, and hard cider. Who does not remember also the coonskin brigade of

Georgia, the coonskin caps, the rollicking coon and " 'possum " hunts of the South?

One of the most terrible incidents in the early history of the colony happened at Cat Island. Duroux, the governor, an exacting tyrant, frequently stripped his men naked when they displeased him, and left them all night on Cat Island exposed to the mosquitoes and sand-flies. His men mutinied and killed him, but they were captured ; one of them was broken on a wheel, and one placed alive in his coffin and his body sawed in two.

It is said that a pirate's ship was wrecked on Cat Island, and that it now lies in the sand deeply buried. Sand storms have blown over and covered it, but sailors affirm that now when a storm rages, the lost souls of the pirates are heard wailing through the wind.

An amusing incident is told as to the manner in which the Isle au Pois derived its name. When the French were encamped there, they were attacked by "small flies or cousins" (mosquitoes), and they fled in such panic that they forgot and left their bag of peas on the island. They could successfully compete with other nations on land and sea, but the mosquito was too much for them.

The history of Dauphine Island is as closely

of the Southern Gulf Coast.

interwoven with the early settlement of Louisiana as that of Ship Island. In 1701, Bienville
received instructions to transfer the seat of
government from Fort Maurepas, at Biloxi, to
Mobile, and Dauphine Island became to Mobile
what Ship Island had been to Biloxi—its place
of anchorage and supply station. Gayarré
tells us that when the French reached the isl-
and they found it covered with bones, and realized that some awful tragedy had been en-
acted there, "but tradition, when questioned,
lays her choppy finger upon her skinny lips,
and answers not." From finding these skele-
tons the island was first called Massacre Island,
but it was afterward changed to Dauphine, in
honor of the Count of Dauphine, who ceded
his province to the French monarch. In com-
pliment to him, the wife of the eldest born son
of the King of France was called Dauphine,
and her husband the Dauphin.

During the first thirteen years of its struggling existence, the little colony was often
pinched by want and absolute famine. Sometimes they were reduced to the necessity of
eating acorns, and several times Bienville scattered them among the Indians to prevent
actual starvation.

Bienville was the second governor, Sauvolle

having been the first. Chivalric, brave, wealthy, and talented, Sauvolle had loved and been loved by one of the noblest women of the court of Louis the Fourteenth, but suddenly there came to him the terrible realization of a great physical trouble. Grief-stricken, he gave up his love, the brilliant court, and all that was dear to him, to face the dangers of the new country and calmly wait the end that heart trouble was likely at any time to bring to him. He died in Biloxi and was buried there.

Dazzled by a knowledge of the treasures of gold and silver found by Pizarro in Peru and Cortez in Mexico, the French sought vainly for mines only. They remained dependent on the mother country, and were blind to the riches of earth and air around them.

While our ancestors were starving in their search for gold, the Indians were enjoying the following appetizing cuisine, as described by Claiborne: Tom-ful-la was their favorite and standing dish. It consisted of corn soaked in lye to take off the husks, then thoroughly boiled with bear's oil, and sometimes the kernels of walnuts and hickory nuts. They barbecued a slice of turkey breast, venison, and bear meat together. They likewise pounded walnuts and hickory nuts, passed them through boiling water, and then through strainers of fine basket work, and this produced a liquor the color and consistency of cream, and of rich and fine flavor.

In 1708, after nine years existence, there were only about three hundred people in the colony, and they had the most meager possessions. In his charming book, the Romances of Louisiana History, Gayarré has not only given us history, but he has touched those rugged times with poetry, and written of them with "a quill dropped from cupid's wing." In this chapter are given glimpses of his pathetic romances of Sauvolle and Crozat; also, the attractive romances of Bienville, Boisbriant, and the Petticoat Insurrection, with their quaint phases and humor.

In 1705, in a ship sent by Louis XIV, were twenty girls who had been carefully selected by the Bishop of Quebec from irreproachable families in Paris. While he had not intentionally deceived them, they came impressed with expectations of a rich and splendid country, but they found immediately the hardships and dangers of pioneer life. In a few months, when the provisions brought by the ship were exhausted, they were reduced to a sole diet of corn. Even in those early days, Paris led in artistic fashions and tastes, and the Parisian girl longed for her dainty surroundings and even a few bon-bons. The Petticoat Insurrection began against the corn diet. They declared that the Bishop of Quebec had deceived them, and that they would leave at the first opportunity. Like sensible, true women, however, they reconciled themselves to the situation, and bravely endured their part of the hardships.

The number of these girls was wholly inadequate to supply the demand. They were lodged in a house to themselves, and during the day they were selected by the French bachelors, but at night a sentinel was placed at the door. Dumont tells us that the last one left was any thing but beautiful—in fact, looked more like a guardsman than a girl. But so great was the desire of these men for homes and domestic happiness that a fight for her possession was imminent. The commandant hearing of it, required the rivals to draw lots for her.

The colony languished until 1712, when it was leased to the great French merchant, Anthony Crozat, for fifteen years, with extraordinary privileges. His principal obligation in return was to send every year to Louisiana two ship-loads of colonists, and after nine years to assume all the expenses of the government. Around this period in the history of the little colony Gayarré weaves one of his prettiest romances.

Crozat had been the son of a peasant, but he was foster-brother to one of the greatest patricians of France. His foster-brother became his benefactor, educated him, and secured for him a fine position in a commercial house. He married his employer's daughter, and after his death, with his wife's inheritance and his own brilliant successes, he became one of the wealthiest merchants of France. His wife and only child, a daughter, were his idols, and when his wife died his whole heart was centered on his daughter—refined, frail and beautiful as a lily.

The dowager Duchess, touched with the loneliness of the motherless girl, asked her to visit her palace. There the beautiful Andrea learned to love, with all the intensity of her being, the sole heir to all these princely possessions, but he was soon betrothed to another equal to him in rank and station. When the preparations for the nuptials began, heartbroken, Andrea returned to her father and he learned the secret of her love. Almost crazed with this great grief in her life, he determined to do the one thing

that could prevent the marriage. It was believed that the noble girl who was to marry
the son of his foster-brother loved another;
equal to her in rank, he could not wed her
because his patrician estate was hopelessly
bankrupt. Crozat went to him, gave him a
royal sum, and told him that it was due to
his estate from an injustice of many years ago.
In bewildered surprise the sum was accepted,
and he married the woman he loved and who
loved him. Then Crozat confessed to the
dowager Duchess and told her of his daughter's breaking heart. The Duchess listened
in stern sadness, but it was impossible! While
she loved the beautiful Andrea, the difference
in rank was too great, nor could Andrea marry
her son unless her father "was a Medici, a
ruler of provinces, and had a historical name."

Crozat thought of the new country, with its
untold riches and boundless territory, and determined to risk every thing for the happiness
of his child. Such is the romance of Crozat's
possession of the small colony on the seaboard. If Gayarré confesses to giving the
story a few touches of his imagination in re-
gard to Andrea's name, her death and that of
her father after the failure of the enterprise,
the story is not the less pathetic, and prob-

ably quite as authentic as many other historic records.

Cadillac was the first governor appointed by Crozat, and the selection could not have been more unfortunate. He was utterly lacking in diplomacy, and was narrow-minded and arrogant. Crozat had promised to him a share of the profits from any mines that he would discover, and his patrician poverty was only exceeded by his avarice. Iberville, Sauvolle and Bienville had received and welcomed each friendly demonstration from the Indians, and treated their customs with respect. When Iberville landed at Biloxi the Indians rubbed his face with white dirt in testimony of their friendship; but when Cadillac was sailing up the Mississippi river and the Natchez Indians offered him their calumet, he scorned to touch with his lordly lips a pipe that had been in the mouth of an Indian. A few days after this the Natchez killed four Canadians; they could not understand Cadillac's manner, and believed it to be a delaration of war.

The word calumet is derived from the Norman word *chalumeau*, and signifies the reed or rustic pipe smoked by Norman peasants. The French introduced the word into Canada.

A most unique Indian masquerade party

was given in the early days of the colony, and combined within itself all the elements of comedy and tragedy.

In order to impress the Indians with the magnificence of the French court, a party of them was induced to visit Paris. Among them was the daughter of the Illinois chief. She was very beautiful, and loved the commander of the French fort in the country of the Illinois.

There was also with the party that went to France a young sergeant, Dubois. The French court received their novel visitors with enthusiastic welcome. A deer-hunt was planned for the warriors at the Bois de Boulogne, and the Indian maidens were toasted, feted, and were the belles of the hour. The Indian princess was converted to Christianity, and at court her marriage with Dubois was celebrated with brilliant pomp, and the king appointed Dubois captain and commandant of the Illinois country. All of the party were loaded with presents, and returned to New Orleans delighted with themselves and their entertainers.

Dubois and his Indian bride seemed to be happy for a time; but she wearied of her civilization masquerade, and longed more and more for the freedom of forest life. Finally she entered into a conspiracy with her tribe, and the members of the French garrison, including Dubois, were massacred. The savage instinct was irrepressible.

With the first Natchez war is interwoven another romance of those early days, but it is a story of love, disappointment, revenge, and the fury of a woman scorned. Cadillac, in his churlish arrogance, made discord with every element around him, and, jealous of Bienville's popularity, was especially antagonistic to him.

Cadillac nad a daughter, but alas! she was not fair, having in face and figure inherited her father's qualities; but she looked upon Bienville's noble face and stately form, and felt that it would be sweet to lean upon his strong arm during those troublous times. Her heart went out more than half way to meet him. Cadillac considered the situation, and, thinking that such a marriage would be an advantage to him, sent for Bienville and made the offer of marriage to him. Astonished and amused, Bienville declined it. Then was Cadillac's small soul lashed into a fury of revenge. He determined to destroy Bienville, and again sending for him, ordered him with a force of thirty-four men to attack the Natchez

and avenge the death of the four Canadians.
Bienville protested that with such a force it
would be impossible, but Cadillac's law was
like that of the Medes and Persians.

Bienville started with his little company, and
determined to do by strategy what he could not
accomplish by force. This was in 1716. He
first went to an island in the Mississippi, op-
posite the Tunicas and eighteen leagues below
Natchez. Pretending to wish to trade with
them, he captured the " Great Sun " and his
two brothers, the " Stung Serpent " and " The
Little Sun." By his treaty with them they
agreed to build a substantial fort at Natchez.
While Iberville, Bienville, Tonti and others
had visited this place before, and occasionally
hunters had settled there, this may be regarded
as the first permanent settlement of the beautiful city of Natchez. It was named Fort
Rosalie in honor of the Countess Pontchartrain. Thus Bienville ended the war without
bloodshed, founded Natchez, and defended the
citadel of his own heart.

This was not the first time during Bienville's
life on the seashore that Cupid had sent his
hurtling arrows above his head. The first en-
counter, however, was not of such a personal
nature.

In 1705, when Louis the XIV sent over the twenty girls, they were chaperoned by a widow, charming and irresistible, as widows always have been and always will be. Major Boisbriant, Bienville's cousin, lost his heart to her, and his was not a case of unrequited love. All went smoothly until Bienville's strong opposition stemmed the current. Major Boisbriant yielded, but the lady, with woman's indomitable will, remained firm and indignant. La Salle and the Curate de la Vente had given Bienville much trouble by their intrigues and slanderous reports of him at court, and now the aggrieved widow added her words of indignant protest. In a letter to the prime minister she writes of Bienville's tyranny in every department, and especially her own wrongs. She annihilates him with this closing sentence : " It is therefore evident that he has not the necessary qualifications to be governor of this colony." He was, however, retained as governor, and the marriage did not take place. Still, we see the early independence of the women of this country, and that they soon became not only a social and domestic, but also political element.

When the French girls came over they found formidable rivals in those first women of

Romance and Realism

Old French Quarter.

the South who dwelt by the sea. The French and Canadians sought them for wives, and who can wonder when we read Claiborne's description of them: "The dusky maidens of Mississippi, with their flashing eyes and voluptuous forms, their delicate hands and feet, and their raven hair that brushed the dewdrops as they walked, modestly drooping their glances at the approach of a warrior. The Choctaw language was beautiful, and some of the women sang well, their voices low and sweet, corresponding with their gentle manners and modest deportment. But they were gay, social, fascinating, and their laugh like the ripple of a brook over its pebbly bed."

After reading this description who can wonder that if the conqueror took from the Indian girl her lands and her wild, sweet freedom, he often gave her in return for it his true, chivalric love?

It is a misfortune of life that the step of realism often touches so close upon the heel of romance, that it crushes out the flowers of imagination. As we see the Indian of the present day, listless, dull, swarthy and slouchy, sitting in the French market, the thought involuntarily presents itself, did poetry throw over those early days the halo of romance, or has civilization only given to the poor Indian its physical enervation without supplying the mental qualities to withstand its temptations?

CHAPTER III.

In 1717, Bienville was reappointed governor, and the seat of government was moved from Mobile and Dauphine Island to Biloxi. As the old fort had been burned at what is now called Ocean Springs, New Biloxi was built upon the point of land to the west of the bay immediately fronting Ship Island.

In March, 1718, Bienville selected the present site of New Orleans between what are now Canal and Esplanade streets, and set fifty men to clearing away the trees. Owing to the differences of Bienville and Hubert, the seat of government was not transferred to New Orleans until 1722, after which this city gradually became the Paris of the South. The French were devoted to the mother country, and felt that it was infamous when, in 1763, Louis XV induced his cousin, Charles III, of Spain to take Louisiana off his hands. So indignant were the French against Spanish dominion that in 1768 they rebelled against it, but they were defeated and their leaders executed. This is one of the darkest tragedies of Louisiana history.

Afterward, however, the Spanish rule was very lenient and just. Governor Gayoso and Governor Galvez were especially beloved, and Governor Miro was so popular that when Tennessee was settled, the central portion of the state was named for him. In the treaty of peace between Great Britain, Spain and France, the Spaniards acquired New Orleans, but the greater part of the Mississippi seaboard was ceded to Great Britain and prospered under British rule. Governor Galvez, however, afterward recaptured it.

Spain was not unwilling when she ceded her Louisiana territory to France by the treaty of Ildefonso in 1800. She feared for her Mexican possessions, and thought France would be a rampart between her and the United States.

Although New Orleans was so long under the dominion of the Spaniards, the Spanish language was spoken officially only, the French being retained for social and family circles. Although loyal citizens of this country, the French have never given up their language as Spaniards, Germans or Italians have done under like circumstances.

Much information is gained on these subjects from Mr. Alcée Fortier, professor of French language and literature in Tulane University, New Orleans. He tells us that so generally was the French language spoken in Louisiana that in the legislature of the state, there was a regular interpreter appointed for each house at a salary of $2,000; it was his duty to translate, if required, the speeches and motions of the members. It was, it seems, very amusing to see a creole representative abusing an American colleague, who remained perfectly unconcerned until the interpreter translated the hostile address; then the party attacked would suddenly rise and reply in vehement terms, which had also to be translated before the opposing member could reply.

The court rooms were provided with French, English and Spanish interpreters, and the juries divided as evenly as possible between English and French. When the case was being presented in English, the French were excused, and when it was argued in French, the English were excused. Together they retired to the jury room, and by some marvelous process generally arrived at a correct verdict.

The creoles of Louisiana are the white descendants of the French and Spanish colonists, and have in their veins some of the blue blood of the noblest families of France and Spain. The depreciatory light in which Mr. George W. Cable has represented them in his works has aroused their just indignation. Dr. W. H. Holcomb says of them: "These men were the root stock or foundation head of the creole civilization, a social state distinguished for the courage and honorable bearing of its men, the beauty and refinement of its women, and the highly polished manners of both sexes."

The pretty quadroon girls who wait in the hotels on the southern seacoast claim with perfect equanimity that they are creoles. This is somewhat bewildering to strangers and a very unjust reflection of color on the subject. Possibly no word in the English language has been more abused than the word creole.

The names of many places in this region are not only historic, but have a story within a story. The French name Baton Rouge not only indicates French possession, but it tells an Indian story. The Houmas, after they had won a victory over the Tunicas, planted upon that spot a "baton rouge," or "red stick," to signify that the Tunicas were never to cross it on the war-path.

Louisiana was named for the French king,

and the two large lakes near New Orleans for two prime ministers—Pontchartrain and Maurepas. Pontchartrain, a man of great talent and sterling integrity, was chancellor of France under Louis XIV. Maurepas, minister of Louis XV, was a man of great ability, but dissolute habits. Pearl river was so called because there the Indians found the shells with which they scraped out their canoes after burning them, and within these shells they often found beautiful pearls. Yazoo river means the "river of death," and Amite river was so named because there Iberville found the Indians most friendly.

One of the first names given by the Spaniards to the Mississippi river was "The River of the Holy Ghost;" other Spanish names were Rio Grande, Rio Esconnido; La Salle first called it St. Louis, and afterward Colbert; La Palisade was one of the French names, from the number of snags and drift-wood in the passes at the mouth of the river. Malbou-chia was the name given to it by the Indians of the East, but the Indians of the West called it Me-ac-cha-sippi, Me-she-o-be, Mec-a-she-ba, and Meche Sepe, all signifying the Father of Waters.

Justin Winsor tells us that the original spelling of Mississippi, the nearest approach to

the Algonquin word, is Mêché Sébè, a form
still commonly used by the Louisiana Creoles.
Tonty suggested Miche Sepe ; Father Laval,
Michisepe, which by Father Labatt was softened into Misisipi.   Marquette added the first
s in Missisipi, and some other explorer added
a second s in Mississipi, as it is spelled in
France to-day.   No one known who added a
second p in Mississippi, for it was generally
spelled with one p when the United States
bought Louisiana.

Free navigation of the Mississippi, a much-
vexed question, was granted in 1795, and the
first steamboat came down the river in 1811.

There is not, perhaps, in the history of Mississippi, a name that graces its pages more
than that of Claiborne.   It has always been
an honored one.   Governor Claiborne had
been governor of the Mississippi Territory, but
when Orleans Territory was formed in 1804, he
was appointed its governor, and appointed first
state governor of Louisiana in 1812.   In 1810,
the Mississippi seaboard was divided into the
parishes of Biloxi and Pascagoula, and the year
afterward Governor Claiborne sent Dr. Flood
to establish these parishes.   A good idea of
the sea-shore at that time may be gathered

from his communication to Governor Claiborne :

" In compliance with your instructions, I embarked in the Alligator on the 5th, and proceeded to Mr. Simon Favre's, on the eastern bank of Pearl river. He is a planter, owns a large stock, and is an educated and very agreeable gentleman. He accepted the commission with pleasure, and will make an energetic officer, and seems greatly to value the respect you have for him. I hoisted the flag of the United States at Bay St. Louis on the 8th, and handed the commission to Phillip Saucier, a venerable gentleman of prepossessing manners and with a patriarchal appearance. Next day, displayed the flag at the Pass, and proceeded to the Bay of Biloxi, where I found Mr. Ladnier and gave him the commission. He is a man of excellent sense, but can neither read nor write, nor can any inhabitant of the Bay of Biloxi that I can hear of. They are all along this beautiful coast a primitive people of mixed origin, retaining the gayety and politeness of the French blended with the abstemiousness and indolence of the Indian. They plant a little rice and a few roots and vegetables, but depend for subsistence chiefly on game and fish. I left with all

these appointees copies of the laws, ordi-
nances, etc., but few laws will be wanted here.
The people are universally honest. There are
no crimes. The father of the family or the
oldest inhabitant settles all disputes. The
population of Pascagoula parish is about 350;
of the parish of Biloxi, 420, chiefly of French
and Creoles. A more inoffensive and inno-
cent people may not be found. They seem to
desire only the simple necessities of life and
to be let alone in their tranquillity."

But the Mississippi seaboard has caught the
spirit of the times, and feels surging through
its every vein the nervous life and progress
of the Nineteenth Century. Not so, however,
with all the people of the coast, for there is
still a people in Louisiana charming in primitive simplicity. As Charles Dudley Warner
tells us, the peculiarity of this community is
in its freedom from all the hurry and worry
and information of modern life. For them the
customs and knowledge of 1755 are quite sufficient, and while some of them are cultured
men and women, the majority can neither read
nor write, considering that this especial phase
of the worry and information of modern life is
unnecessary.

In 1605, a small French settlement was

made in Nova Scotia—the word Acadian is derived from the word Aquoddie, an Indian term for a fish called the pollock. These people were of exquisite simplicity of character and habits.

"Thus dwelt together in love these simple Acadian
    farmers,—
Dwelt in the love of God and man. Alike were they
    free from
Fear, that reigns with the tyrant, and envy, the vice of
    republics.
Neither locks had they to their doors, nor bars to their
    windows;
But their dwellings were open as day and the hearts of
    their owners;
There the richest was poor and the poorest lived in abun-
    dance."

They were most loyal in their devotion to France, but when they passed under the reign of the English this loyalty was feared, especially as their numbers increased alarmingly. Finally they were expelled by the English from their beautiful homes, and, penniless and heart-broken, drifted along the Atlantic shore. Many places gave them homes, but the dearest spot discovered by them was the beautiful country near New Orleans watered by the Teche. There they were welcomed with generous hospitality; there they found their own language, a genial climate, and rich soil.

Longfellow has immortalized the sufferings of the Acadians in his beautiful poem of Evangeline—Evangeline, the daughter of Benedict, and Gabriel Lajeunesse, the son of Basil the blacksmith. Separated from her love in that dreadful eviction from their home, for years she vainly sought him; vainly sought him in the fair Louisiana country:

" 'Sunshine of Saint Eulalie' was she called; for that was the sunshine,
Which, as the farmers believed, would load their orchard with apples.

. . . . . .

He was a valiant youth, and his face, like the face of the morning,
Gladdened the earth with its light, and ripened thought into action.

. . . . . .

Far asunder on separate coasts the Acadians landed.
Scattered were they, like flakes of snow, when the wind from the north-east
Strikes aslant through the fogs that darken the banks of Newfoundland.
Friendless, homeless, hopeless, they wandered from city to city.

. . . . . .

Sometimes she lingered in towns, till, urged by the fever within her,

46

Urged by a restless longing, the hunger and thirst of the
    spirit,
She would commence again her endless search and en-
    deavor;
Sometimes in churchyard strayed, and gazed on the
    crosses and tombstones,
Sat by some nameless grave, and thought that perhaps in
    its bosom,
He was already at rest, and she longed to slumber beside
    him.
Thus did that poor soul wander in want and cheerless dis-
    comfort
Bleeding, barefooted over the shards and thorns of ex-
    istence.

.   .   .   .   .

But Evangeline's heart was sustained by a vision, that
    faintly
Floated before her eyes, and beckoned her on through the
    moonlight.
It was the thought of her brain that assumed the shape of
    a phantom
Through those shadowy aisles had Gabriel wandered be-
    fore her,
And every stroke of the oar now brought him nearer and
    nearer.

.   .   .   .   .   .

Filled was her heart with love, and the dawn of an open-
    ing heaven
Lighted her soul in sleep with the glory of regions ce-
    lestial.

.   .   .   .

Nor that day, nor the next, nor yet the day succeeding,
Found they trace of his course, in lake or forest or river,
Nor, after many days had they found him.

.   .   .   .   .

Gabriel was not forgotten. Within her heart was his
    image,
Clothed in the beauty of love and youth, as last she be-
    held him,
Only more beautiful made by his deathlike silence and
    absence.
Into her thoughts of him time entered not, for it was not.
Over him years had no power; for he was not changed
    but transfigured;
He had become to her heart as one who is dead, and not
    absent;
Patience and abnegation of self, and devotion to others,
This was the lesson a life of trial and sorrow had taught
    her.
So was her love diffused, but, like to some odorous spices,
Suffered no waste nor loss though filling the air with aroma.
Other hope had she none, nor wish in life, but to
Meekly follow with reverent steps the sacred feet of her
    Savior.
Thus many years she lived as a sister of mercy; fre-
    quenting
Lonely and wretched roofs in the crowded lanes of the
    city,
Where distress and want concealed themselves from the
    sunlight
Where disease and sorrow in garrets languished neglected.
  .   .   .   -   .   .

All was ended now, the hope and the fear and the sorrow,
All the aching of heart, the restless, unsatisfied longing,
All the dull, deep, pain, and constant anguish of patience!
And as she pressed once more the lifeless head to her
    bosom,
Meekly she bowed her own, and murmured, ' Father, I
    thank Thee.' "

A charming little book, "In Acadia," by Margaret Avery Johnston (Mrs. William Preston Johnston), gives a complete picture of the Acadians.

In striking contrast to them were the Baratarians who lived on the southern coast of Louisiana. The story of one is like a still fair landscape with softly floating clouds above it; that of the other like the rushing, seething waters of Niagara, carrying every thing before its strong current; one wanted little here below, the other reached out its grasping hands for all the luxuries of the earth; the romance of one was instinct with the gentlest passions that could stir the human heart, the romance of the other was a dare-devil recklessness and thrilling adventures—for the Baratarians were the followers of the Lafitte brothers, the bold buccaneers and terrors of the sea.

Barataria really included all the gulf coast between the Mississippi river and Bayou LaFourche, but the home of the Lafittes was on the beautiful island of Grand Terre on Barataria Bay. Miss Grace King gives us the possible derivation of the word: It will be remembered that Barataria was the name of the island presented by the frolicsome duchess to Sancho Panza for his sins as he learned to

remember it. How or when the name came to
Louisiana is still to be discovered, whether directly from Don Quixote or from the source
which supplied Le Sage with it; the etymology
of the word *Baratean* meaning *Barato*, cheap
things.

When Lafitte was outlawed and a reward offered for his capture, under an assumed name
he accidentally met Madame Claiborne, and so
charmed was she with the fascinating stranger,
that when she returned to the Governor she
was most enthusiastic.

Grand Terre is now deserted except, as Laf-
cadio Hearn beautifully describes it, by "a
whirling flower-drift of sleepy butterflies."

Cable tells us that in 1795 New Orleans was
nothing but a market town. The Cathedral,
the Convent of the Ursulines, five or six cafes,
and about a hundred houses were all of it.
Only two dry-goods stores—pins, $20.00 a
paper, and poor people had to use thorns
for pins. A needle cost 50 cents, stock-
ings $5.00 a pair, postage on a letter 50 cents.
The fashions and etiquette allowed only silks
and velvets for visits of ceremony, and though
you smothered you obeyed these tyrannical
laws!

Many amusing stories are told of the great

formality of those early days, but at the same
time there was often blended with it a humorous brusqueness and frontier independence.
Claiborne gives us a story of camp-life : In
1798 the first United States troops that came
down the Mississippi were quartered at Fort
Adams. Gen. Wilkinson, Col. Hamtramck,
Maj. Butler, Capt. Green and other officers
were merry over their punch one night, and the
general by some accident got his queue singed
off. Next day he issued an order forbidding
any officer to appear with a queue. Major
Butler refused to obey, and was put under ar-
rest. Soon after he was very sick, and when
he knew he could not live he made his will, and
gave instructions for his burial, which he knew
would be attended by the whole command.

" Bore a hole," said he, "through the bottom
of my coffin right under my head, and let my
queue come through it, that the d—d old rascal may see that even when dead I refuse to
obey his order." These directions were liter-
ally complied with.

That early period was not characterized by
the freedom of action and speech which is now
enjoyed by our Republic. When the struggling colonists demanded of Cadillac that all
nations should be allowed to trade freely with

them, and that when they were dissatisfied they could move out of the province, he was most indignant. He wrote an angry letter to the Prime Minister saying: "Freedom of trade and freedom of action! A pretty thing! What would become of Crozat's privileges?" Fortunately, however, all the governors of that time were not Cadillacs.

Having given a chapter to the Indians, we now reach a class of people much nearer to us, and that will most probably remain in Dixie so long as there is a cotton row to be followed by a negro, a plow and a mule. The very mention of the South brings visions of white cotton fields and looming above them the woolly heads and shiny teeth of the darkey. The responsibilities of life weigh more heavily upon him now, and his laughter is not so frequent as it used to be; but his sunny disposition is a heritage of the tropics, and he will always be happy and improvident.

Before entering upon this subject a few words are due to King Cotton, the staple of the South. Immediately upon the seacoast the atmosphere is rather too damp for its production, but a few miles inland and the Mississippi valley produces the finest grade of cotton, making New Orleans one of the largest cotton-shipping ports of the world. A variety of cotton seed is used in Mississippi, but for many years one of the most popular was the Mexican seed. This was introduced into the United States by a diplomatic ruse, it is said. The story is told that Gen. Wilkinson sent Walter Burling of Natchez on a diplomatic mission to Mexico in 1806. He dined with the viceroy and requested some Mexican seed, but as this was against the Mexican law, the viceroy declined. He told Mr. Burling laughingly over his wine, however, that he could take as many *Mexican dolls* as he wished, and it was tacitly understood that these dolls should be stuffed with cotton seed.

In 1708 Bienville wrote to the government to obtain authority to exchange Indians for negroes. "We shall give," said he, "three Indians for two negroes. The Indians, when in the islands, will not be able to run away, the country being unknown to them, and the negroes would not dare to become fugitives in Lousiana because the Indians would kill them." This does not seem to have met with any favorable consideration, and the proposition reflects no credit on a man of Bienville's fine character The entire ring of it makes an unpleasant impression.

When Crozat gave up his lease in 1717, the

Romance and Realism

Avenue of oaks.

West India Company leased it for twenty-five years, and in the charter bound itself to introduce 3,000 Africans. Thus early in the history of New England, Virginia and Louisiana the blight of slavery was imprinted on the colonies. In July, 1720, the first cargo of negroes came.

No humanitarian could advocate slavery, and there was doubtless pathetic physical and mental suffering on those terrible slave ships. We should remember, however, that these simple, ignorant blacks were taken from their homes of absolute darkness and superstition, and that many "Mars Chans" and "Meh Ladies" were waiting on these southern shores to hold them in such gentle bonds and teach them such loving service, that they forgot that they were slaves.

Slavery has existed in some forms in all ages; but nowhere upon the pages of history do we find any thing like the tender, inexplicable and devoted bond between the Southern master and his slave.

In that sweet long ago what Southern child could forget the delight of a visit to "de quar-. ters"—the rows of nicely whitewashed negro cabins near the white house. There our devoted hosts bustled around with noisy hospitality, drawing down from the loft some of their

treasures of hickory nuts, walnuts, and other
goodies; roasting eggs for us in the ashes,
giving to us risen pone corn-bread and fresh
vegetables—for every cabin was provided with
its little patch of ground at the back. And
the little piccaninnies rolled over each other on
the floor, like black kittens, a sable heap of
delight

"Oh, de cabin at de quarters, in de ole plantation days,
   Wid de garden patch behine it an' de godevine by
      de do',
   An' de do'yard sot wid roses, whar de chillun runs an
      plays,
      An' de streak o' sunshine, yaller-like, er slantin' on
      de flo'!"

As for mammy, such a thing as rebellion
against her was almost undreampt of, for she
was high in authority. The lessons that she
taught us in good manners were correct in the
extreme, for had she not been "'mongst de
white folks long 'nuff ter know?" Some of
the other lessons that she taught sank deep in
childish memory.

You must always burn and not throw
away your hair, because the birds will pick
it up to make their nests, and that will
make you crazy. If a child teething looks at
himself in the mirror his teething will be pain-

ful. If you have a sore on the tip of your tongue it is a sign that you have lied. If you forget what you were going to say, it is a sign that you were going to lie. If you sweep the feet of a child with a broom, it will make him walk early. To cure a wart take a green pea, rub it on the wart, then take the pea and wrap it in a piece of paper and throw it away; the person who will pick it up will get the wart. You must watch for a full moon if you want to make soap. In those days, if the smiling but determined mothers had not asserted their authority and trimmed their babies' finger nails, they would have grown out like little birds' talons and scratched their tender faces. The nurses always insisted that to trim the nails would make the child steal.

The greatest terror was felt of the will-o'-the-wisp. We were told that so surely as we should go out of the yard after dark, without a grown person, this unknown fiendish spirit would catch us and drag us over bogs and through bushes, exclaiming all the time, " I have you! I have you!"

All such stories had a perfect fascination for the children, and the more startling their character, told by these black mammies in the flickering firelight or by the ghostly moonlight, the greater was the shuddering delight which they produced.

Southerners are not more superstitious than other people, and they show their wonderful strength of character in throwing off these numberless superstitions that they absorbed almost with their first breath of intelligence from these devoted attendants.

Mr. Fortier mentions all of these superstitions and many more in his "Louisiana Studies," and his description of New Year's Day, on the southern coast, gives such a vivid and charming scene of plantation life in Louisiana, that it is repeated in full:

"At daylight, on the first of January, the rejoicing began on the plantation; every thing was in an uproar, and all the negroes, old and young, were running about, shaking hands and exchanging wishes for the new year. The servants employed at the house came to awaken the master and mistress and the children. The nurses came to our beds to present their *souhaits*. To the boys it was always, 'Mo souhaité ké vou bon garçon, fé plein l'argent é ké vou bienhéreux;' to the girls, 'Mo souhaité ké vou bon fie, ké vou gagnin ein mari riche é plein piti.'

"Even the very old and infirm, who had not

left the hospital for months, came to the house with the rest of *l'atelier* for their gifts. These they were sure to get, each person receiving a piece of an ox killed expressly for them, several pounds of flour, and a new tin pan and spoon. The men received, besides, a new jean or cottonade suit of clothes, and the women a dress and a most gaudy handkerchief, or *tignon*, the redder the better. Each woman that had had a child during the year received two dresses instead of one. After the *souhaits* were presented to the masters, and the gifts were made, the dancing and singing began. The scene was indeed striking, interesting and weird. Two or three hundred men and women were there in front of the house, wild with joy and most boisterous, although always respectful.

"Their musical instruments were, first, a barrel with one end covered with an ox-hide— this was the drum; then two sticks and the jawbone of a mule, with the teeth still on it— this was the violin. The principal musician bestrode the barrel and began to beat on the hide, singing as loud as he could. He beat with his hands, with his feet, and sometimes, when quite carried away by his enthusiasm, with his head also. The second musician took the sticks and beat on the wood of the barrel, while the third made a dreadful music by rattling the teeth of the jawbone with a stick. Five or six men stood around the musicians and sang without stopping. All this produced a most strange and savage music, but, withal, not disagreeable, as the negroes have a very good ear for music, and keep a pleasant rhythm in their songs. These dancing songs generally consisted of one phrase, repeated for hours on the same air.

"In the dance called *carabiné*, and which was quite graceful, the man took his *danseuse* by the hand, and made her turn around very rapidly for more than an hour, the woman waving a red handkerchief over her head, and every one singing—

'Madame Gobar, en sortant di bal,
Madame Gobar, tignon li tombé.' .

"The other dance, called *pilé Chactas*, was not as graceful as the *carabiné*, but was more strange. The woman had to dance almost without moving her feet. It was the man who did all the work, turning around her, kneeling down, making the most grotesque and extraordinary faces, writhing like a serpent, while the woman was almost immovable. After a little while, however, she began to get excited, and, untying her neckerchief, she waved it around gracefully, and finally ended by wiping off the perspiration from the face of her *danseur*, and also from the faces of the musicians who played the barrel and the jawbone, an act which must have been gratefully received by those sweltering individuals.

"The ball, for such it was, lasted for several hours, and was a great amusement to us children. It must have been less entertaining to our parents, but they never interfered, as they considered that, by a well-established custom, New Year's Day was one of mirth and pleasure for the child-like slaves."

Nothing in the world could so terribly frighten a negro as the thought of being "hoodooed," and the real voudouism was something to be feared. It was a knowledge of the subtle vegetable poisons brought from Africa by the negroes, and which always meant slow death to their victims. They prayed to the devil, for they considered him God, and their dances and religious rites in secluded places were frightfully grotesque. A great deal of voudouism, however, was simply ridiculous and harmless ceremonies. Mr. Fortier tells us that one of his friends, passing a house late at night, saw on the doorsteps two lighted candles and between them four nickels placed as a cross. Being determined to save the family from destruction, the gentleman blew out the candles, threw them away, and pocketed the nickels. Thus all danger was averted.

Louisiana negroes pride themselves upon their superiority over the ordinary negro, because many of them have straight hair. This is due, however, to the fact that in the early days of the colony there were many Indians and negro slaves working together, and the two races became intermixed. When there was a mixture of white blood with the negro the different grades were known as mulatto, quadroons, octaroons and griffes.

In the terrible insurrection of the blacks against the whites in San Domingo, 1791, a large number of San Domingans found refuge in Louisiana, some bringing slaves. The Louisianians felt the greatest anxiety for fear that this might cause an uprising by their negroes, but there was never any serious trouble on their account.

Under the Black Code before the civil war, masters were compelled to care for their slaves when disabled by old age or sickness. If the master failed to do this, the slave was sent to the nearest hospital, and the derelict master was taxed so much a day for his support; and if he failed to pay, the hospital had a lien on his plantation for that amount.

The principle of slavery, however, was acknowledged to be wrong, not only by the North, but by the South. The trend of Southern thought and legislation was the liberation of the negro, but it was a stupendous subject, which time alone could have peacefully solved.

In the revised constitution of Mississippi of 1832, a remarkable clause prohibited the introduction of slaves as merchandise or for sale from and after May 1, 1833. This was when slaves were most remunerative. In the Constitution of the Confederate States, the slave trade was forbidden.

If the North and the South had waited only a little longer; and had they not made the terrible mistake of thinking that war was the only way of settling the question, brother would never have been arrayed against brother. The heroes in the blue and in the gray would never have shed their life-blood, and the voice of lamentation would not have been heard all over the land.

CHAPTER IV.

NEW ORLEANS.

One of the first poetical names of New Orleans was Houma, or Sun. The Parisian has transformed this weed-covered marsh, with its trees draped in melancholy gray moss, into a brilliant garden filled with flowers and optimistic life, for to him life means laughter, lightness and love.

When the marshy streets were impassable with mud, it was not sufficient cause to prevent joyous reunions. Upon raised planks on the banquettes the families went forth—first a slave preceding them with lanterns, next another slave bearing the satin slippers and other articles of full dress that were to be donned in the dressing-room, and last came the family. If the evening was too inclement for the ball, a crier went through the streets and announced it to the sound of a drum, and it was always understood it would take place the next pleasant evening.

Later, when pavements permitted the luxury of carriages and when theaters were built, the regular evening outfit for a fashionable cavalier was: a stall for four, white kid gloves for the ladies, coffee for the party, or perhaps a more expensive supper at a restaurant. When the Opera House was opened people were considered out of the bounds of cultivated society unless they attended the theater or opera several evenings during the week, and at any hour of the day or evening there came through the windows that always stood open, soft refrains from the opera—not alone from the stately drawing-rooms, but from the streets and the slave quarters. All the air seemed vibrant with melody. And meeting some of the family servants in the French Market, you were greeted with a quaint curtsey, a happy smile, and perhaps a quotation from Shakspeare—household words in the families in which they served, and all spoken in French.

How vividly these scenes contrast with the early customs of the Pilgrim fathers in Boston! One all life and light and color; the other stern, rugged strength, based upon the austerest form of religion. Had the varied elements that composed the New Orleans population landed in Boston, the dignified calm of that place would have been shaken and shocked to its inmost center.

Romance and Realism

To the western Parisian, the picturesque, the dramatic, and the poetic were inherent characteristics, but it was only at times that his butterfly wings carried him into an excess of frivolity. His heart and his home were open to the refugees of the earth, wherever they were persecuted and unfortunate.

There were no blue-coated police, but the watchmen of New Orleans were arrayed in gorgeous uniforms, and sang forth the hours of the night and the state of the weather until the rhythmic cadence echoed from street to street: "Eight o'clock and fair." "Nine o'clock and cloudy." In the winter, a cannon was fired at eight o'clock, and in summer at nine o'clock, for all subordinates to go to their homes, and after that time all slaves and stragglers were required to show passes from their masters and employers.

On the streets, you met "haughty *habitans* fresh from Canada, rude trappers and hunters, *voyageurs* and *coureurs de bois;* plain, unpretending Cadians from the Attakapas, arrayed in their home-made blue cottonades, and redolent of the herds of cattle they had brought with them; lazy emigre, nobles banished to this new world under *lettres de cachet* for interfering with their king's petit amours or taking too deep an interest in politics; yellow sirens from San Domingo, speaking a soft, bastard French, and looking so languishingly out of the corners of their big, melting, black eyes that it was no wonder that they led both young and old astray, and caused their cold, proud sisters of the *sang pur* many a jealous heart-ache; staid and energetic Germans from the 'German Coast,' with flaxen hair and Teutonic names, but speaking the purest French, come down to the city for supplies; haughty Castilian soldiers, clad in the bright uniform of the Spanish cazadores; dirty Indians of the Houma and Natchez tribes, some free, some slaves; negroes of every shade and hue from dirty white to deepest black, clad only in the *braguet* and shapeless woolen shirts, as little clothing as the somewhat loose ideas of the time and country permitted."

Not the least important of this varied group were the Kaintucks, who floated down the river in their flats or broad-horns, sold their merchandise, and received for it huge rolls of money, which they proceeded at once to spend with convivial generosity. They felt that there were but few persons more lordly than themselves; few to whom they should doff their coonskin caps. With bowie-knives and pistols

stuck above their leathern breeches, it is small
wonder that, at their approach, the pompous
watchmen sank into the depths of their gorgeous uniforms, and neither saw nor heard
any depredations upon the quiet of the hour.
There was this difference between the Kaintucks and Rex, who now annually enters the
city—if the keys of the city were not turned
over to them, they took possession of them
with perfect good-humor, and held high but
harmless carnival for a few days. Then, as
now, the Kentuckian carried with him his
pluck and energy, his independence—and his
corkscrew.

The free speech of the present newspaper
reporters would not have accorded with the
rigid customs of those times. It was safer
then to indulge in glittering generalities, for
the slightest personalities, the least reflection
upon one's honor, called forth a flash of the
rapier, or notes were exchanged, and at day-
break next morning two quiet-looking carriages
rolled out to the Oaks, or to some other duel-
ing-ground near the city. The pen refuses to
linger upon the tragedies of this subject, for
there were dark and desperate tragedies that
chilled the heart; but as one of God's greatest
blessings to us in life, some of the most somber

subjects are often relieved with touches of sentiment and humor.

All the world loves a lover, and all the world loves a fighter, and the duel often combined the two. Innumerable romances are connected with this subject. The story is told that a beautiful Creole girl loved a noble cavalier, but while her heart thrilled to his every touch and word, his ardent devotion was repaid with capricious frowns, and to others she gave her smiles and favors. One night, at a ball, she accidentally learned that he was to fight a duel at sunrise the next morning, but not by a single word did she betray to him her knowledge of this, and with the perversity of a woman's heart, she yielded not to the pleadings of his softened voice. She was the gayest of the gay until at three o'clock she bade him good-bye, the flush still on her cheek, the brightness of her eye undimmed—then she drew around her trembling shoulders her white opera cloak, and waited for the dawn. With the first ray of light, her ball dress unchanged, she sprang into her carriage and bade her coachman drive to the Oaks. Then, sending him a short distance away, she stood in the shadow of the trees, white and motionless as a statue, the beating of her heart almost stilled

with its agony of suspense. They came, and
with the first shot her lover fell. She sprang
forward, and the brilliant luster of her eyes
held the intensity of a lifetime ; the spirituelle
pallor of her face, the indescribable grace of
her swaying body, the small satin slippers
stained with grass, the silken robe trailing in
the dew, the bare white arms and shoulders,
upon which the jewels still gleamed—all
formed a beautiful picture, in startling contrast
with her grewsome surroundings. But even the
endearing tones of her voice seemed to have
the power of calling back his fleeting spirit,
for the surgeon discovered a faint throb of life,
and having him tenderly put into her carriage,
she carried him to the city and nursed him
back to life and happiness. The citadel of
woman's heart may seem impregnable, but
when the sweet surrender comes at last, it is
complete and absolute.

There were many duels in which there was
no woman at the bottom of the case, nor in
any way connected with it, though this may
be doubted by cynical bachelors and other
people equally agreeable.

Fortunately, in all cases, the first blood
drawn was sufficient to appease wounded
honor. In many cases the seconds arranged

matters so that dignity and honor were protected without fatalities, and the Sketch-book, replete with charming information of New Orleans, gives one quaint instance where the principal was quite capable of caring for his honor and saving his own life. The affair was between Mons. Marigny, who belonged to one of the oldest families of Louisiana and Mr. Humble. Marigny was sent to the Legislature in 1817, at which time there was a very strong political opposition between the Creoles and the Americans, which provoked many warm debates in the House of Representatives and the Senate. Catahoula parish was represented by a Georgia giant, an ex-blacksmith named Humble, a man of plain ways but possessed of many sterling qualities. He was remarkable as much for his immense stature as for his political diplomacy. It happened that an impassioned speech of Mons. Marigny was replied to by the Georgian, and the latter was so extremely pointed in his allusions that his opponent felt aggrieved and sent a challenge to mortal combat. The Georgian was nonplused.

"I know nothing about this dueling business," said he, "I will not fight him."

"You must," said his friend. "No gentleman can refuse."

"I am not a gentleman," replied the honest son of Georgia, "I am only a blacksmith."

"But you will be ruined if you do not fight," urged his friends, "you will have the choice of weapons, and you can choose in such a way as to give yourself an equal chance with your adversary."

The giant asked time in which to consider the question, and ended by accepting. He sent the following reply to Mons. Marigny:

"I accept, and in the exercise of my privilege, I stipulate that the duel shall take place in Lake Pontchartrain, in six feet of water, sledge hammers to be used as weapons."

Mons. Marigny was about five feet eight inches in height and his adversary was seven. The conceit of the Georgian so pleased Mons. Marigny, who could appreciate a joke as well as perpetrate one, that he declared himself satisfied, and the duel did not take place.

The Place D'Armes, now Jackson Square, was the commercial and social rendezvous of the town. Upon its sward the merriest gatherings were held; there the itinerant merchant vended his wares, affairs of state were cele-

Jackson Square and St. Louis Cathedral.

brated, or the gibbet loomed its ghastly frame, or criminals were placed alive in coffins, nailed up, and slowly sawed in two. It was in front of the cathedral, government house and calaboose, and adjoining the Halle de Boucheries, or old French Market house.

The last name applies to the present market house, because it is on the site of the first one used in New Orleans by the French. For years it has been one of the most charming attractions of New Orleans, with its picturesque costumes and booths, its babel of languages, its café noir, its Indians and quadroons, its varied nationalities and novel commodities. All this is gradually disappearing before the possession of the thrifty, practical American, who wears plain clothes and looks like any other plain man, talks plain English, and sells plain market articles, just as you would find them in any other plain American markets. It is somewhat of a shock to know that a new market house, with all modern improvements, is planned for the old site. One feels tempted to protest against such an innovation, and to go out into the highways and hedges and engage a few Indians and foreigners to stay a little longer with their shrill but delightful jargon and their quaint wares.

of the Southern Gulf Coast.

It is in just such places as the old French
Market that we would, if possible, stay the
foot of progress. To improve and modernize
it is like taking one of the pictures of the old
masters and freshening it up with a little new
paint.

The Cathedral is perhaps dearer to the New
Orleans people than any other building, and
inseparably connected with the history of the
place.

The present building stands on the same site
where several others have been burned, or
destroyed by storm—the first house having
been a simple shed, when the population was
not more than two hundred. The present
building was erected in 1792 by one of the
most remarkable characters who ever lived in
New Orleans, Don Andres Almonaster-y-
Roxas. His body rests under the altar, a
marble slab is inscribed to his memory, and
there every Saturday mass is said for the re-
pose of his soul. Besides building the Cathedral, he founded the St. Charles Hospital
and its chapel, the chapel of the Lazarists, the
chapel of the Ursulines Convent, a hospital
for lepers, schools for little children, the Pres-
bytery of the Cathedral, and many other chari-
table institutions.

His daughter, the Baroness Pontalba, was scarcely less conspicuous in the history of New Orleans. Her wealth, style of living and life sounds like a leaf from fairy land. When she went to Paris with her husband she bought the beautiful palace containing four hundred rooms, built by Louis XIV for the Duc du Maine, but she afterward built a smaller but just as magnificent palace for herself. She and her father-in-law, Baron Pontalba, disagreed painfully, and one morning they were found in his library, he quite dead, and her body with many bullet wounds in it. She was at first supposed to be lifeless, but lived for many years afterward. The mystery of the scene was never explained.

The picturesque delights of plantation and town life can be appreciated by giving two scenes from Miss Grace King's charming work, " New Orleans, the Place and the People."

" It certainly was worth traveling fifty miles to hear Mademoiselle Macarty described by the nonagenarian historian Gayarré and see one of her visits to his grandmother, Madame de Boré, acted. Her carriage, a curiosity in the colony, was called a chaise ; it was like a modern coupé, but smaller, with sides and front of glass. There was no coachman. A postillion rode one of the spirited horses, a little black rascal of a postillion, who always rode so fast and so wildly that his tiny cape stood straight out behind him like wings. When in a cloud of dust the vehicle turned into the Pecan avenue, the little darkies stationed there would shriek out in shrill excitement to get the announcement to the great gates ahead of the horses, 'Mam'selle Macarty a pé vini,' and there would be a rush inside to throw the gates open in time. And his cape flying more wildly than ever, his elbows beating the air more furiously, the postillion would gallop his horses in a sweeping circle through the great courtyard, and bring them panting to a brilliant finale before the carriage steps. Mons. de Boré would be standing there with his lowest bow to open the carriage door and hand the fair one out, and lead her at arms' length with stately minuet step up the broad brick stairs and through the hall to the door of the salon, where they would face each other, and he would again bow and she would drop a curtesy into the very hem of her gown—her Louis XIV gown—for from head to foot she always dressed in an exact copy of the costume of Madame de Maintenon ; that is, all to her arms, which

were in Mademoiselle Macarty's youth so extremely beautiful that she never overcame the
habit, even in extreme cold weather and old
age, of exhibiting them bare to the shoulders.
The mystery why with her great wealth and
her great beauty she had never married remained a vivid one—even when old age had
effaced every thing except the fame of her radiant youth."

Not less attractive was Miss King's picture
of town life: " The early rising and cup of
coffee; the great court yard stretching open
for all the breezes and all the world that chose
to enter; the figs, pomegranates, bananas,
crape myrtles, and oleanders glittering in the
dew; the calls in the street, musical negro
cries heralding vegetables, fruits, and sweets;
'Belles des figues!' 'Tout chauds! Tout
chauds!' 'Barataria! Barataria!' 'Confitures
coco!' 'Pralines Pistache!' 'Pralines Pecanes!'
the family marchande coming into the courtyard swaying her body on her hips to balance
the basket on her head, sitting on the steps to
give the morning news to the family sitting
around the breakfast table on the gallery; the
dining-room on the *rez de chaussée* and opening
into the street for all passers by to see, if they
would, the great family board (for there were

of the Southern Gulf Coast.

no small families in the ancient regime) and
the pompous butler, and the assistant ' gardi-
enne' in bright head handkerchief, gold-hoop
earrings, white fichu and gay flowered gowns!''

Even the pralines sold on the street have a
history. Made into large disks of brown sugar,
pecans, cocoanuts or peanuts, they are delicious.
Many dyspeptics have been tempted and
tempted again, until the memory of the dainty
confections became one of painful pleasure.

It is said that a nobleman banished from
France landed in New Orleans, dependent
alone upon his wits, but these did not fail him.
He bought a few pounds of sugar and some
pecans, and established the first of those popular stands now seen on so many street corners
of the city. He had a wonderful dog who ex-
amined the picayunes that were given in and
threw out those that were counterfeit, and an
equally wonderful monkey whose tricks were
not less attractive. Crowds flocked to his
stand, and his empty coffers were soon filled.
In the day time he was the street merchant,
but in the evening he was the courtly nobleman, and, donning his *costume de rigueur*, he
was welcomed into the most elegant homes,
and his brilliant bon mots quoted every-where.
With his pralines he amassed a fortune. A

sudden change in the political situation of
France—for France sometimes has these little
changes—restored to him his title and vast
estates.

New Orleans is a city of magnificent distances. It is 187 square miles or 119,680
acres, but not over one-tenth of this is inhab-
ited. The reason that the city limits are so
immense is that it is necessary to have this
country under municipal law for drainage. The
geographical center of the city is a dense
swamp, but, when a picture of it was taken and
sent to a northern magazine as the heart of
the city, the editors declined to accept it, saying that the public would not believe such
representation to be true.

There are two seasons in New Orleans pe-
culiar to the place: Mardi Gras is a season of
unbounded revelry and joy, but All Saints
Day—les jours des morts—is consecrated to
the dead.

In the early days of the colony many of the
young people were sent to Paris to be educated, and from that place, in 1827, was introduced the custom of celebrating Mardi
Gras. It seemed peculiarly appropriate that
Louisiana should celebrate Mardi Gras, as
Iberville and Bienville landed in Louisiana on

Mardi Gras Day. The first floats used in such celebrations originated in Mobile in 1831 by the Cowbellians, and floats were not used in New Orleans until 1857. Rex did not enter the city until 1872, when he came attended by a body guard of Arabs.

It was on the occasion of the visit of the Grand Duke Alexis, and since that time he has come regularly. To Rex the keys of the city are given, and all the people are his most loyal subjects until the last notes of the carnival die away with the dawn of Ash Wednesday, when he mysteriously disappears until the next year's carnival. Mardi Gras is one of the many joyous occasions of New Orleans, for the Frenchman believes that this life is worth living, and fails to adopt the Scotchman's stern creed: " You'll be damned if you do, and you'll be damned if you don't."

There are several organizations devoted to Mardi Gras, the oldest being the Mistick Krewe, Twelfth Night Revelers, Knights of Momus, etc. During the year they are busy for the next celebration, but all in the profoundest secrecy. To appreciate the splendor of Mardi Gras, it must be seen. It is simply magnificent tableaux representing the finest works of prose and poetry: Lallah Rookh,

Mythology, Spenser's Fairie Queen, Homer's Tale of Troy, the Romance of Mexico, Mother Goose's Tea Party, the Birds of Audubon, and too many others to mention.

On All-saints Day the streets, carriages, street cars, and every conceivable vehicle, seem to be moving flower gardens. Every one is laden with flowers—dried immortelles made of curled, glazed, white, black and purple paper, fragrant flowers covered with sparkling dew, anchors, hearts, crosses and wreaths—all wending their way to the city of the dead. There, for days previous, the scene has been a busy one. On account of the marshy nature of the soil—water being very near the surface—the dead are generally buried above ground in receiving vaults, one above the other. The lots, however, are cleaned of every withered leaf and twig ; each lot has its workers, and outside the city gates the scene is a busy one. There are venders of sand, grass, garden tools, even coffee booths—every thing that could be needed by the workers.

At midnight it is said the dead arise, and shaking off the cerements of the grave, greet each other and are free until the dawn. Then, in their narrow homes, they wait for their loved ones, for they know that they will come laden with flowers. If in the rush and necessities of life during the past year they may at times have been forgotten, it will not be so to-day, for the day is theirs. Loving tears will be given to them, and the tender murmured words will speak only of their virtues, for their faults will be forgotten. And when the shadows of evening come they will be left covered with beautiful flowers and tenderest remembrance. At each gate a nun stands with orphans beside her, and their appealing baskets are filled with coins by the passing crowd.

If New Orleans is one of the gayest of all cities, it is also one of the most devout. The Ursuline Convent, established in 1727 by Louis XV, is the oldest building in the Mississippi valley, and the oldest convent in the United States. Of the rigid order of the Discalced Carmelites there are only four in the United States, one being in New Orleans. When a nun enters this order she is buried to the world, and her face is never seen again save by her sisters in prayer. Eight hours of the day are given to the church service, and their fast is only lightly broken from the 14th of September until Easter. Their bare cells contain only a chair, a table, and a bed made by resting two planks on rude benches; these planks have a little straw on them, and their only covering is a sheet of serge. They flagellate their tender bodies until the blood sometimes falls. For permission to have a drink of water they must ask the mother superior, and the granting of this request is often postponed if the mother thinks patience can stand self-denial a little longer. At night their supper is two ounces of bread measured out to each—the weight of four soda crackers—with a little tea or wine. They desire to suffer as Jesus suffered in the world, and by their prayers and penance these lovely, living saints endeavor, in a measure, to expiate the sins of the world.

Where the famous quadroon balls were given there is now a colored convent. The subject of the quadroons is one of the saddest of all the minor chords of love and suffering in the history of New Orleans. These beautiful women, with their liquid dark eyes, their rich complexions tinged with brilliant color, their graceful figures, gleaming jewels and elegant dresses, won the devotion of ardent admirers and wrecked the happiness of many homes. But a change came over the spirit of the times. The quadroon balls ceased to exist, but the beautiful women still lived, knowing

that their white blood lifted them far above the
negro circles, and that their negro blood closed
against them the social circles of irreproachable standing. In anguish of spirit they felt
that in all the wide world there was no resting
place for their weary feet. But the church,
with divine compassion, forgave them for a sin
that was not theirs, and enfolding many of
these sinless souls of a sinful love in her protecting arms, they found purity, usefulness and
happiness in a convent.

Where music and dancing once sounded,
there is now the noiseless footstep of the nun;
where the beautiful, restless eyes once told
of weary hearts, there is now the benediction
of peace; and where the siren's voice once
lured to destruction, the nun's murmured prayer
lifts the struggling soul heavenward.

New Orleans also has its ghost stories,
especially that of the Haunted Exchange.
This house was once the scene of hospitable
elegance, its wealthy mistress a leader in
every public enterprise. For years, however,
she secretly treated her slaves with the utmost
cruelty. So little was any thing of this kind
tolerated by the people, that, when it was discovered, an indignant mob rushed to the
house, threw the costly ornaments into the

street, and only the dismantled walls were left standing. The terrified mistress escaped by a back street, where a carriage was waiting, and fled to France, from which place she never dared to return.

The house is still pointed out to strangers, and, in low tones and with many significant glances, the story is told that no one who has ever lived there has prospered since that night of righteous indignation. The writer, however, has recently visited the place, and found the occupants looking like people who eat and sleep with good average comfort. Neither did they seem disposed to unfold any tales that would harrow the soul and make "each particular hair to stand on end."

History opens her pages of interest to us, but it is not more charming than the object lessons of the past received from varied architecture, monuments, and names of streets. Even the epitaphs of the cemeteries speak in silent but eloquent language of the great ones of church and state, or the lowly ones in their humble walks of life who have helped to make the history of the place; its varied language tells of the successive possession of French, Spanish and American, or the tie of love between master and slave. Nothing could be more simple and touching than an epitaph in Girod Cemetery: "Mammy, aged 84; a faithful servant. She lived and died a christian."

After the disastrous fires of 1780 and 1794, the temporary French frame houses were superseded by the substantial Spanish houses with their tiled roofs, their quaint balconies jutting far over the streets to be socially near their neighbors across the way, their great open courts, odd windows, and all that goes to make the picturesque.

In his book, "The Manhattaner in New Orleans," Oakey Hall was most enthusiastic over the names of the streets in New Orleans, and pronounced them more beautiful than those of any other city in the Union. They mark the progress of the city step by step. Ursuline tells us of the arrival of the good nuns in 1727, the first real educators of the city; Hospital street, the founding of the hospital; the Napoleonic craze was marked by the names of a number of streets—Napoleon avenue, Jena, Austerlitz, and a number of others. In their love for the classics, any number of Greek and Latin names were adopted. They captured all the Muses and Graces, but their names are so filtrated through French pronunciation that Parnassus itself could scarcely recognize its representatives.

The monuments of the city are not all cast in bronze and marble in cold commemoration of the dead, but many of them are the homes for the living, the sick, and suffering; or they open the halls of knowledge to the struggling masses, and give them footholds into higher walks of life. And around some of these buildings are woven such stories of romance that we forget the realism of their brick and mortar, and through and through they become to us palaces beautiful.

To John McDonogh the public schools owe untold gratitude, and yet his life was one of bitter disappointment, and his days were spent in sorrow and isolation. When a young man, he came from Baltimore to New Orleans, and his elegant bachelor home was the center of gayety and refinement. He loved and was beloved by a beautiful accomplished girl, but she was a Roman Catholic and he was a Protestant, and her parents were unyielding in their opposition. She joined the Ursuline nuns, and he closed his beautiful home and became a business automaton. There was only one bright spot to him in each year as it passed—when she became Mother Superior of the Convent, he with others was allowed on New Year's Day a brief, ceremonious call. So entirely did he deny himself all the luxuries of life that he was often slightingly mentioned as a miser.

But his soul was not slumbering, for when it winged its flight from the worn-out, discrepit, and lifeless body, a will was found with tenderest provision for the poor and needy. His vast wealth was divided between the schools of Baltimore and New Orleans, and a pathetic clause in his will asked that little children would come and lay flowers on his grave once a year.

Judah Touro also loved and was beloved, but the objection of her family was insurmountable. `He buried his broken heart in a life of active business and broad charity. To himself he denied every luxury, but to the needy his purse was open. For the Dispersed of Judah he built a magnificent synagogue, the ground alone costing $60,000. The Touro Infirmary cost $40,000; he gave $20,000 to the Bunker Hill monument, $40,000 to the Jewish Cemetery, at Newport, Rhode Island, and any number of other charities.

Every city has its examples of transition from poverty to wealth, or from wealth to poverty, but for these changes of fortune New Orleans seemed to have an underlying current of sentiment peculiarly her own.

Julian Poydras commenced his career in New Orleans with a pack on his back, yet in a few years he entertained at his home, with royal magnificence, Louis Phillippe, Duke of Orleans, and his party, and it is said he furnished the exiled prince with money. At his death he left twelve hundred slaves, with instructions that they should be freed—this, unfortunately, however, was never done. He founded the Poydras Asylum, a college for indigent orphans, and gave innumerable other charities. To several parishes he bequeathed $30,000, the interest of which was to be given each year to the dowerless young girls who married during the year. Mr. Poydras was never married, but who can tell what tender memory may have dwelt in the heart that received this poetic inspiration to give to others that sweetest of all blessings—dearer than fame, dearer than wealth—domestic happiness.

In New Orleans was erected the first statue in the United States to a woman—and that woman was simply a washerwoman, a dairy woman and baker—who drove her own cart and delivered her goods at back doors, and

Drive on the beach.

could neither read nor write; but when she died, the highest dignitaries of the city honored her memory, and her statue in its homely attire, was placed in front of one of the orphan asylums that she had befriended.

The orphans of the city were in great need, and in her cart she gathered every-where food and old clothes for them, and she gave to them with lavish generosity from her small earnings; but the more she gave the more fortune seemed to smile on her, until her bakeries grew from small beginnings to immense profitable establishments, and all the orphans of the city considered her their best friend.

There are several varieties of that being poetically described by Rudyard Kipling, as "A rag, a bone, and a hank of hair." Some are pieces of delicate, beautiful bric-a-brac intended only for parlor ornament; some are utterly without ornament, but with hearts that radiate sunshine all about them, and with strong shoulders that not only bear their own burdens, but those of the helpless and dependent. Such a woman was Margaret Haughery, and there is no name enshrined with more reverence and respect in the hearts of New Orleans people than that of this lowly but wonderful philanthropist.

of the Southern Gulf Coast.

It is impossible to mention all the charming
incidents of New Orleans in one chapter, nor
to dwell on its many elegant clubs, its regattas,
its sports, its universities, libraries, public
buildings, nor its many wonderful characters.
It was here that Adah Isaacs Menken commenced her brilliant checkered career; here
that Paul Morphy lived, the champion chess
player of the world, who received in London,
Paris and elsewhere royal ovations; and in
New Orleans was commenced the wonderful
law suit of Myra Clark Gaines. which dragged
its slow length along for many years.

To history is left the details of the exultant
welcome given to the hero of Chalmette, and
the despair and disorder of New Orleans when
in 1862 Farragut entered it. A city of burning cotton, its fine docks at Algiers destroyed,
its gutters running with molasses, its stores
opened for the people to help themselves, in
order that such supplies should not fall into the
hands of the enemy. Nor shall we dwell on
that period after the war when the noble state
of Louisiana was given over to the rule of the
carpet-bagger and the negro—when the state
hall of the old St. Louis Hotel that had
echoed to the silver-tongued eloquence of
refinement and culture resounded to corn-field

lung power, of which the following is a sample: "Dat de gen'l'm from de parish of St. Quelquechose was developing assurtions and expurgating ratiocinations clean agin de fust principles of law and equity."

CHAPTER V.

BEAUVOIR AND THE MYSTERIOUS MUSIC OF THE SEA.

The sea-coast has felt each heart-throb of the nation's history. She has welcomed to her shore the heroes of her own and other lands. In the depths of her solitude, brave men have dreamed of the future greatness of this country, and nature has smiled upon their budding hopes, or wept with them over the sere and yellow leaf of their failures and disappointments. Nature is a confidante who never betrays the most exquisite suffering, who never jars us by idle words, but in her own sweet, silent way uplifts, soothes, and comforts.

It is here that the rippling waters of the gulf bring the languor of the tropics to meet the thrifty energy of the North, and here the refugees from San Domingo, France, and all the points of the earth have wept over a past that could not be recalled, or found oblivion of their troubles in renewed prosperity and happiness. Changing with each season, nature

Romance and Realism

Beauvoir.

here is always beautiful—as beautiful now as when, two hundred years ago, La Salle took possession of the lands of Louisiana and the great river in the name of his king, and the cathedral bells of Canada rang out exultant over the fame of his great discovery—bells, however, that soon tolled the news of his death by the assassin's blow. His only heritage of the vast area that he had discovered was six feet of ground as a resting-place; the only earthly possession that the greatest can claim after life's fitful fever is over. The name of the fort of Croeve Coeur testified that when he reached the last days of his long and noble life, he was broken-hearted.

It was here that the youthful Bienville, the father of Louisiana, brought a statesmanship that has not since been excelled, and that taught him to deal successfully with the Indians. Here he fought his battles of victory and defeat, and bore all the hardships of pioneer life, until, calumniated by his rivals, he became broken-spirited and discouraged. In his old age, he turned his reluctant steps to France, but left his heart and dearest hopes with the land of his adoption.

The end of life has often brought to the

great hearts of the earth misconstruction and sorrow.

It has not been many years since these sad sea waves sang the requiem of Southern woe, and soothed the last days of a man who embodied the rise and fall of Confederate hopes— Jefferson Davis.

Beauvoir, with its beautiful view of the sea, is one of the favorite spots of interest to both northern and southern tourists. There are some visitors to Beauvoir frivolous and indifferent, but before the silent grandeur of the place the light laughter and jesting words are hushed. There is an indescribable influence in the stately oaks with their mournful swaying gray moss, the broad verandas with their fluted columns, the silence of the deserted rooms, the white draperies that enwrap furniniture and bric-a-brac and stand around like ghostly phantoms, the books that seem to be falling from the shelves from disuse and old age, the empty chair in which Mr. Davis thought and planned his book, "The Rise and Fall of the Confederate Government," the floating cobwebs, the crumbling plastering and the tangled flower beds and undergrowth.—These teach earth's inexorable law that all things animate and inanimate, exalted and humble, must yield to destruction and oblivion. There is something in the sorrows of a great man which appeals to the latent nobility of every heart, and in all ages the chivalry of the victor to the vanquished has met with the plaudits of the earth, but it is not the object of this little book to enter into the rights and wrongs of the civil war, for Time's obliterating touch is rapidly removing the scars of that unfortunate period.

Even now, in a distressed island, the honor of the United States is jealously guarded by an ex-Confederate General.

With his own hands he has placed the old flag above his couch. At night his last glance rests upon it as dreams of home and native land succeed the anxious responsibilities of the day ; and when morning comes, his first waking glance dwells upon its brilliant folds, and his devotion to it can not be questioned.

In this crisis of his country's history, the great, loyal heart of Fitzhugh Lee knows no sectional lines of North and South, but he does know that a Solid South is ready to rise in defense of the nation's honor.

It had been far better for the world from the beginning, however, had the gates of Janus never unclosed, for when war descends, even upon the most civilized nations, it means desolation, pain and anguish, and the trail of the serpent is over it all.

Soon after the late war, Mrs. Sarah A. Dorsey welcomed to her home, Beauvoir, the Confederate President and his family.

She was a woman of fine mind and generous impulses. She was not only a good historian, but a fine linguist. Brilliant and restless, she had felt an infinite longing all her life for something higher and better than the ordinary routine of life, and in making her home the refuge for a broken heart, she found the peace of a mission fulfilled.

Her friendship for Mrs. Davis had begun in their schooldays, and alternately they acted as amanuensis for Mr. Davis in preparing the first volume of his book.

As the home of Mr. Davis, Beauvoir became the Mecca of the South and a spot of greatest interest to the North. Visitors from all sections of the United States were received with a simple hospitality that befitted his fortunes, and the refined, cultivated atmosphere of his home gave to it an indescribable charm. It was most natural that Mr. Davis's friends should be enthusiastic over him, but the following sketch of him has been given by the historian, Mr. James Redpath, a lifelong political opponent:

"He seemed the ideal embodiment of sweetness and light. I never heard him speak an unkind word of any man. His manner could best be described as gracious, so exquisitely refined, so courtly, yet heart-warm. The dignity of most of our public men reminds one of the hod-carrier's 'store suit.' Mr. Davis's dignity was as natural and charming as the perfume of the rose—the fitting expression of a serene, benign, and comely moral nature."

One rare characteristic he possessed, which should have recommended him to his strongest opponents: it is said of him that "he was an orator who gave close attention to the necessity of stopping when he was done." Many brilliant men, from time immemorial, have been unable to stop when they were done, whether it was a flight of oratory, a social call, or any of those pleasant scenes in life when a little would be most bright and restful, and a little too much would be most witless and burdensome.

The life of Mr. Davis was one of strange and romantic vicissitudes. At West Point, he was the classmate of R. E. Lee, and when the

Black Hawk was begun, it is said that at Fort
Snelling he administered to Abraham Lincoln
his first oath of allegiance to the United
States. In that wild frontier life, these two
young men, who were afterward to figure so
conspicuously in the history of their country,
learned the art of Indian warfare, and saw an
eagle's feather added to a warrior's head-dress
for each scalp he took. There they went to
the gumbo balls of Wisconsin, where a bowl
of gumbo and an ample slice of bread constituted the refreshments, and an old-fashioned
fiddle furnished the music, and gave more
pleasure than is often given now by a full or-
chestra to tired revelers.

The tragic death of Mr. Lincoln was a great
misfortune to the South. Genial and kind-
hearted, he had shown a desire, after the surrender, to be just to that section of country.
The man who had so long dwelt in the shadow
of stage tragedy sent a thrill of horror through
the North and South by his last acting.

Both Mr. Lincoln and Mr. Davis were
social and possessed a keen sense of humor,
and to Mr. Davis especially this was a buoy-
ant comfort in the last scenes of his life.

An appeal to the humorous side of his
nature was almost irresistible, as instanced by

the following note received during one of the darkest periods of the war:

Dear Mr. President:—I want you to let Jeems C. of Company Oneth, South Carolina Regiment, come home and get married. Jeems is willin', I is willin', his mammy says she is willin', but Jeems' Captain he aint willin'. Now, when we are all willin' cep'n Jeems' Captain, I think you might let up and let Jeems come. I'll make him go straight back when he's done got married and fight just as hard as ever.

Your affectionate friend, etc.

Mrs. Davis tells us, in her Memoirs of Mr. Davis, that he could not refuse this earnest request from an " affectionate friend."

Much has been said of the reckless extravagance of Southern people, but perhaps this extravagance reached its height during the war. While the thrifty New Englander was giving $5.00 an ounce for quinine, the spendthrift Southerner, in 1865, did not hesitate (when he could get it) to pay $1,700.00 an ounce. He gave from $125.00 to $150.00 for a pair of shoes, $300.00 for a barrel of flour, $3,000.00 for a plain suit of clothes, and

$125.00 for a penknife. A dinner for one man sometimes cost $500.00; but, then, who has not heard of the Southern tables laden with every delicacy that could be desired? At this time the people absolutely seemed to fail to appreciate the value of their money, and sometimes threw it away or burned it. The unique fashions also have never been duplicated before or since. Ladies adopted the custom of wearing shoes made from old sails and carpets; they used parched sweet potatoes, corn or okra for coffee; homespun dresses had never been at such a premium since pioneer days, and silks and velvets were entirely out of style. In fact the description of the eccentric fashions of that time could easily fill a large and interesting volume. Strangely enough for a fashion book, however, it would be one that could only be read 'twixt a smile and a tear.

When the Liberty Bell was taken from Philadelphia to New Orleans, Mr. Davis met it at Biloxi, January 26, 1885. The committee invited him most cordially to go with them to New Orleans, and in response to a speech of welcome Mr. Davis spoke with an eloquence that thrilled his hearers. His little grand-

daughter patted the bell with her tiny hands
and lisped, " God bless the dear old bell."

Mr. Davis died in New Orleans on the 6th
of December, 1889.

One by one, nearly all of the leaders of the
North and the South have answered to the
last call and sleep in their last camping ground.
Perhaps no one has versed these thoughts
more beautifully than Mrs. Margaret Hunt
Brisbane :

"Sleep, brothers, sleep !
Your fame will keep
As fresh and pure as the winds that sweep
O'er ferny fell and fen ;
In whiter tents than we ever knew,
In peace eternal, grand and true,
To-day the fallen gray and blue
Are camped with God."

Very near Beauvoir is the Sea Shore Camp
Ground of the Methodist Episcopal Church.
It belongs to the New Orleans, Mobile and
Sea Shore District Conference. It is quite a
charming place, and has a frontage of 1,400
feet and is two miles deep. This camp ground
proves that the good old customs are not all
obsolete, and who knows but that these soul-
stirring Methodist hymns, as they are carried
far out over the gulf in wave after wave of

sound, are not caught beneath the water and given back to us in that strange, mysterious music of the sea? Some of the old negroes tell that in that long ago when their sea-shore revivals were held, many of their members "came through" with religious ecstacy, and rushing into the sea believed it to be the river Jordan washing away their sins. They say that the sea imprisoned these wild shouts and singing, and that the storms free these sounds and they come back to us in strange, fitful notes.

When we reach the poetic subject of the mysterious music of the gulf, Science bends her knitted brows in thought, and a wild, sweet range is given to the touch of romance. Some of the legends regarding this music are given in the following poem, written by Mrs. Laura F. Hinsdale:

"There is a time when summer stars are glowing,
    And night is fair along the Southern shore,
The sailor resting when the tide is flowing
    Hears somewhere near below his waiting oar
A haunting tone, now vanishing, now calling,
    Now lost, now luring like some elfin air;
In murmurous music fathoms downward falling,
    It seems a dream of song imprisoned there.

of the Southern Gulf Coast.

The legend tells a phantom ship is beating
On yonder bar, a wanderer evermore,
Its rhythmic music, evanescent, fleeting,
Stirs the lagoon and echoes on the shore.
O! phantom ship, dost near that port Elysian
Where radiant rainbow colors ever play?
Shall hope's mirage return a blessed vision,
And canst thou find a joy of yesterday?

The legend tells of a pale horseman fleeing
Whose steed the gnomes with metals strange have shod,
Who on and on, a distant summit seeing,
His way pursues in ocean paths untrod.
His spectral hoofs by the evangel bidden
In far Carillons beat in measure low.
Elusive tone! dost near where that is hidden
Which made the music of the long ago?

The legend tells of sirens of the ocean
That wander, singing, where the sea palms rise,
And through the songs intense and measured motion
I seem to hear their soft imprisoned sighs.
They lure me like the spell of a magician—
Once more I see the palaces of Spain,
I feel the kindling thrill of young ambition—
The tide sweeps on, the song is lost again.

The legend tells of vocal sea sands sifting,
With vibrant forces, resonant and strong,
And on the surging sand-dunes fretting, drifting,
Like broken hearts that hide their grief in song.
Tell me, white atoms, in your sad oblation
Of drift that lies so deep that none may scan,
Is it forgotten in God's great creation
Who formed the fleeting hour-glass life of man?

The legend tells of those who long have slumbered,
    A forest race too valorous to flee,
Who when in battle by their foes outnumbered
    With clasping hands came singing to the sea.
The ocean drew them to her hidden keeping,
    The stars watched o'er them in the deep above—
Their death lingers, but the tones of weeping
    Tell the eternity of human love."

This last verse embodies the sweetest, saddest, and most generally accepted of all the legends. This music is heard more distinctly at Pascagoula than any other point on the coast. The sound is like that of an Eolian harp when stirred by a soft, gentle wind. This is the pathetic story of the Pascagoula tribe:

It was one of the most powerful on the seacoast, and ruled over what is now Pascagoula, Scranton, and Moss Point. Olustee, the son of the chief, while hunting, met Miona, the daughter of a neighboring chief, and together they learned the sweet old story. Olustee begged that she would come to his people and be the light of his wigwam, but with tears she told him that her father had pledged her to the fierce Otanga, the chief of the Biloxis. Her love for Olustee, however, proved to be greater than her fear of her father, and, yielding to his entreaties, she fled with him to Pascagoula.

Coosa, his father, the great chief, was charmed with her beauty, sweetness, and grace, and the next day, 'midst the rejoicing of the tribe, the nuptials were to take place. The wrathful Otanga heard of the flight of his bride, and joining her father, they fell that night upon the sleeping tribe of the Pascagoulas. Bravely the latter fought, but Olustee, seeing that his tribe was about to be conquered, begged that they would deliver him to the enemy, as he had been the cause of strife, but Miona said:

"Otanga wants but me,
And, as this bloody war was for my sake,
Give me to him, and he will leave thee free."

The brave warriors swore, however, that they would either save their chieftain and his bride or perish with them in the sea; that their tribe should never be in subjection to the hated Biloxians. And so, when all hope was lost, squaws and children led the way, the braves followed with chants of victory, and all plunged into the sea. The last victims, after a tender embrace, being Olustee and the beautiful Miona. Together they went to the Happy Hunting Grounds.

Bienville heard this music of the sea, and records it in his narrative; but neither poetry

nor science has yet discovered the Rosetta
stone by which the mystery can be solved.
In the Popular Science Monthly (April, 1890),
Mr. Chas. E. Chidsey has an article on the
mysterious music of Pascagoula. He ad-
vances the theory of Darwin and Charles
Kingsley as to similar music heard on the
southern coast of France. In his "Descent
of Man," Darwin says: "The last point
which need be noticed is that fishes are known
to make various noises, some of which are described as musical. Dr. Dufossé, who has
especially attended to this subject, says that
the sounds are voluntarily produced in several
ways by different fishes; by the friction of the
pharyngeal bones; by the vibration of certain
muscles attached to the swim bladder, which
serves as a resounding board, and by the vibration of the intrinsic muscles of the swim
bladder. By this latter means, the Trigla
produces pure and long-drawn sounds, which
range over nearly an octave. But the most
interesting case for us is that of two species
of Ophidium, in which the males alone are
provided with a sound-producing apparatus,
consisting of small, movable bones with proper
muscles in connection with the swim bladder.
The drumming of the Unbrinas in the Euro-

pean seas is said to be audible from a depth
of twenty fathoms, and the fishermen of Ro-
chelle assert that the males alone make the
noise during spawning time, and that it is possible, by imitating it, to take them without
bait." Prof. G. Brown Goode, in his "Amer-
can Fishes," mentions several species to which
the name "drum" has been given, because of
their ability to produce sound.

But who would believe that this dream of
song comes from a drum or any other kind of
fish, when we can enter the vast realms of fancy
and learn that it is sound from a phantom ship,
or the echo from the spectral hoofs of the pale
horseman's steed as he pursues the oceans
paths, or that it is the siren's alluring voice
or imprisoned sighs, or that it is the vocal sea
sands drifting, or the lament of Indian romance?

Like a mirage from the past, tradition brings
to us visions of romance and adventure with
every step that we take upon this enchanted
shore. Even the flowers distill their fragrance
with memories of the past, and the white
Cherokee rose bends and blooms as sweetly
now as it did in that night of long ago, when
its soft radiance illuminated the pathway of the
good Father Davion. Lost in the tangled

Romance and Realism

depths of palmetto and swaying reeds, he vainly sought the pathway to Fort Louis. At last the light from a Cherokee encampment gleamed upon him, and there he found refuge. That night he prayed long and earnestly that he might be restored to his people. Sleep came and

"In a dream he saw once more his mother's tender eyes
Bending above him in the light that fell from Paradise."

Pointing to a snow-white flower, she told him that it would lead him to his home. In a pathway of light the roses descended from Heaven to earth, and above them he saw among the stars, the Master's crown of thorns.

Waking, he found, with joyous wonder, the flowers blooming around him, and extending far into the depths of the forest. Ever before him they sprang up to mark his pathway—

"Follow," they seemed to whisper, "for we are leading thee
Onward and ever onward to the old fort by the sea."

Over white sand dunes they led him, and when swollen bayous were reached, they tangled their tiny tendrils into strong bridges upon which he crossed. On and on they led him until at Fort Louis he heard the joyous welcome of Sauvolle and his comrades. And in.

the forest we still find this Cherokee rose "with its snow-flake petals and heart of golden light."

Sometimes on dark summer nights when moon and stars forget to shine, a soft light descends upon the waters illuminating sea and shore, and the mariner stills the uplifted oar and bows his head in reverential memory of woman's faith and woman's love.

In the early days of the colony, when the little band struggled with disease and hardship, famine stalked into their midst, and, lifting its skinny hand, laid a deadly touch upon its victims. The grand monarch, hearing the voice of his children crying for bread, sent a ship across the stormy waters laden with all that could relieve their distress.

The white sails were about to be unfurled when a beautiful woman, Eona, tearful and flushed, knelt at the feet of her king, and begged that her lover, only yesterday given to her in the bonds of wedlock, should not be sent to this far-away land of unknown trial and danger.

"What!" said the king with reproving glance. "Do you forget his duty as a soldier, and would you unnerve the courage that should rescue the destitute and starving?"

Church of the Redeemer.

The roses faded from her cheeks as she fainted beneath the realization of her sorrow.

With the memory of his kisses still upon her lips, she knelt before the altar in the darkened chapel. Day after day passed, but to her time and earth were forgotten, and her soul was uplifted in agonized prayer for the safety of her beloved. Her little hands clasped upon her breast, became as waxen in their pallor as the white draperies that wrapped her slender, graceful form, the frost of sorrow whitened her raven tresses, and the statue of the Virgin above the altar seemed no purer and motionless than the grief-stricken figure. But when life seemed to have been absorbed in the intensity of her entreaty, music not born of earth floated down upon her; a heavenly peace descended upon her, and a voice of angelic sweetness whispered that there is a love of such holy birth that its radiance can forever light the path of its beloved.

The rescue-laden ship sped on over the vast stretch of waters until she entered the gulf, but when she had almost reached the land, the darkness of deepest night descended upon her. Fear came upon the hearts of the mariners, their cheeks paled, and with startled glance they looked out upon the waters for the dreaded wreckers. The vessel drifted, they knew not where, but suddenly the sea was illuminated with a soft light, and they saw before them the safety of Ship Island harbor.

While joy reigned that the ship was safely landed, that bread was given to the starving, the soldier lover knew that the light of faith had guided them, that the prayer of Eona had enfolded them with heavenly protection.

The day of wreckers has gone, and our land is one of smiling plenty, but Eona's light still comes to prove that love can be lifted above all earthly dross, and that it can live beyond the grave, limitless as time itself.

The legends of the Cherokee rose and of Eona are taken from Mrs. Laura F. Hinsdale's charming little book of poems, Legends and Lyrics of the Gulf Coast.

As a resident of the coast, Mrs. Hinsdale has taken the greatest interest in its beautiful romances.

CHAPTER VI.

The Illinois Central and Louisville and Nashville Railroads have largely assisted in developing the sea coast. Especially the Louisville and Nashville road, as it runs parallel with
the gulf, giving almost a constant view of its
waters, and passing through the main sea
coast towns.

Soon after leaving New Orleans, on the
Louisville and Nashville Railroad, Chef Menteur is reached. Translated into English, the
name means "Lying Chief," and thereby
hangs a tale.

The Choctaws were especially averse to lying, and when one of their chiefs yielded con-
tinually to this habit, they banished him from
the tribe, and he established his home at Chef
Menteur. While the name commemorates
the frailty of one Indian, it speaks in eloquent
terms of the truthfulness of the entire tribe.
The Choctaw of that day was not sufficiently
civilized to acquire the habit of lying.

Past is the day when the Indian lover lighted
his torch, and with beating heart went to the

wigwam of his beloved, to learn his fate. Happiness was to be his if she met him and blew out the light; but keen was his disappointment if she refused to look at the light, and, turning her back upon him, veiled her face with her raven tresses. Past are these days of Indian romance, and passing away are all of the Indians. In the pathetic language of the last chief of the Pottawattamies—in the twentieth century the Indians will be absorbed by the dominant race, and they will follow the buffalo into the land of memories and fables.

In contrast with our own day, the following from the pen of M. W. Conelley embodies much interest of Indian life.

"He loved nature, and was satisfied with it as he found it. He did not deface the earth. He did not alter the physical face of nature. He lived in comfort and at ease, and never subjected himself to high pressure as we do to-day. He did not consume the tribal or natural resources in building levees to control floods. When the waters were flung down upon the lowlands, he reared mounds to the summits of which he ascended, and remained safe until they abated. Where the forests grew he was content to leave them in primeval splendor. He burned the dry grass and small shrubs every year, making of the forest a grand park through which wild deer could be seen feeding, and over which the wild turkey roamed. This forest and the streams which flowed through it were his smokehouse and granary. When he desired food he went out and supplied his needs. He did not take fish from the water or inflict death on wild animals for 'sport,' as does the white man. He did not exterminate for the mere love of destroying life. In his forest temple he worshiped the Supreme Being, and his untutored mind saw God in clouds or heard him in the winds, and the dryads in their trees communed with him. Truly, he was a child of nature. In the red man's economy there were none of those perplexities that vex a higher civilization. There were no strikes or lockouts or boycotts. There were no walking delegates or plutocrats or paupers. There was no land or tariff question or tax question or labor question. High license and prohibition were unknown. There were no new women or social problems or sexual aberrations. No one was ever hunting a job, and the genius of the tramp had not yet developed. The Indian was contented. He demanded and expected no more of life than he could easily obtain.

He had no jails or reformatories, no saloons or other resorts of established reputation. There were no policemen or sheriffs, no courts or combines. The Indian is passing away and will soon be a memory, but the study of his life will be a valuable lesson to those who are being consumed by the fever of civilized conflict."

Near Fort Rosalie, where the Natchez lighted their fires and sang their songs, modern historic romance has chronicled its stories. It was near here that Aaron Burr's flotilla sent a wild thrill of excitement through the country, and his domineering, impatient spirit chafed against the martial and civic restrictions that encircled him. It was here that in the trellised walks and sheltered arbor of Half-way Hill he met beautiful Madeline. Under the influence of his fascinations and the finished polish of his manner, her heart quivered into new life and happiness. On the night of his wild flight, when his horse was stopped beneath her window, and he entreated her to go with him, her innate purity and a mother's protecting love alone saved her from inevitable misery.

But he carried with him her sacred covenant and pledge, from which, however, he released her when he wandered in foreign lands, an outcast, desolate and poverty-stricken.

It was also in historic Natchez that Andrew Jackson wooed and won Mrs. Rachel Robards, *nee* Donaldson. He was married to her at the residence of Thomas Marston Green, in Jefferson county. The soldier who turned a rugged front to English bullets and Indian arrows surrendered to the charms of this sweet woman. She was afterward a source of unfailing comfort in his domestic life, and infinite pride in the attractive grace with which she presided over the high social duties of his position.

The small compass of this book does not permit justice to all the romantic spots upon the coast—the wishing-well of Scranton, the lovers' oak at Pascagoula, the oak that has listened to tender words told in the Indian dialect, in impassioned French, in soft Spanish, or in English. Love enters into all languages, and yet it has been truly said that it has a language of its own whose eloquence needs no words for expression. Love and life are inseparable, for love has lighted the world ever since the example of that first affair in the Garden of Eden.

Romance and history have woven their charms for each place on this balmy shore,

where one "could never find the skeleton
nakedness of leafless forests, the fair earth
resting under a funereal winding sheet of snow,
and the babbling rills and laughing brooks
hushed into frozen silence."

The names of many places link together past
and present associations. Heron Bay commemorates the number of herons found there. Man-
chac means strait or pass, and connects Mississippi River with Lake Maurepas. The name
Chandelier Island was given because discovered
on the day when the Catholic Church celebrated
the feast of the presentation of Christ in the
temple and the purification of the Virgin Mary.
It is flat, sandy and unprepossessing, but noted
for its wonderful bird eggs. The name Pass
Christian tells the story of the Norwegian
sailor who first discovered the deep channel
that is near this point, or perhaps it may com-
memorate the time when the early priests
taught the Indians the first principles of Christianity. Bay St. Louis was so named by Bienville because the French arrived there on the
day of St. Louis, son of the beautiful and vir-
tuous Blanche of Castile. Pass Christian and
Bay St. Louis are two of the most attractive
places on the coast, and especially popular
with the people of New Orleans.

Bois d'Ore means "gilded woods," for there the trees were found resplendent with color. Even the "cow counties" on the coast, Harrison and Hancock, have an association more poetic than the bovines that now roam their fields, for the name originally meant the home of the buffalo—Terre aux Bœufs, or "Land of Beeves."

If time permitted, it would be a delight to linger at each of these seaside towns, that extend almost continuously on the coast, in Louisiana, Mississippi, Alabama, and Florida. The stay, however, in this land of beautiful dreams and realities must end.

As the object of this little volume has simply been the collection of charming romances and incidents of the sea-coast, no effort has been made to mention special places, enterprises, and people. Biloxi is mentioned as a typical town, not that, with all its charms, it has greater attractions than some other places, but it can claim the distinction of having been the first permanent settlement, and, therefore, to it is given the special attention and deference that is due to old age.

The name Biloxi means "broken jar," and it was here that Sauvelle, Tonti, and many of the early heroes found a last resting-place in

Fort Maurepas. Many of the homes retain
the picturesque architecture of the old colonial
period. The progress of the present combines
with the quaint attractions of the past.

One evening, a friend and I planned a visit
to Aunt Eliza, one of the old inhabitants of
the place. She opened the door of her neat
cabin.

"Aunt Eliza," said I, "we are strangers
visiting Biloxi, and came to make you a little
call."

Immediately her black face lighted with
cordial hospitality, and she bustled around to
get chairs for us, dusting each carefully with
her apron.

"Won' you res' yer hats?" said she.

"No; we just want you to tell us something of Biloxi, and what it was years ago,
How long have you lived here?"

"Ever sence I waz jes that high," said she,
holding her hand a little above the floor.
"An' I cum from Ole Virginny, an' my fambly
was the Stevens fambly, on Jeems river, one
uv the fust in the land;" and she bristled with
pride.

It was not long before she began to talk of
religion, for nearly all old darkies are religious
to a morbid degree, but we gently pulled her

wandering remarks back to what was most interesting to us, the past. Soon in speaking of the dizzy gayety of her youth, her religion ebbed slowly into the background.

"Dans! I could cut de pigon wing and out dans de debbil," and she chuckled to herself. "Onct, when Miss Anne hed company, she cum out ter de cabin wid oneuv young mistiss ole party cloes, an sez, 'Liza put thes on yer and thes long gluvs an this mas, an cum inter the settin room an dans ter-night,' an they clap ther hans, an Miss Anne laffed an laffed sorter sof to hersef, kase me an her wuz the onliest ones wat knowed it was little black Liza dan-sin," and the good old soul beamed with delight over this retrospect of the fascinating wickedness of her young days.

Ah! those happy times when the sympathetic bond between mistress and maid radiated happiness on many scenes that are now fading into the dim distance of the past.

In the course of the conversation, Aunt Eliza confided to us that one of the dreads of her life had been that she would have some trouble with a blue gum nigger who might bite her. "Fur," she said, "I'd rather be bit by a rattlesnake than a blue gum nigger." This

is a common superstition with nearly all negroes.

As the Indian estimated time by a bundle of
sticks, so the negro often estimates it by some
tender, sweet association, for instance—

" How old is your boy, Aunt Dinah ? "

" Who, dat Rastus ?   He'll be nigh onto
sebenteen nex watermillion time."

It is characteristic for them to use big words
and always to assume an air of importance in
a court-room.

Judge—" What about this case—have you
a lawyer to defend you ? "

" No, sah."

" What are you going to do about it?   How
will you get along without one ? "

" Well, Jedge, I went out and insulted one,
an he tole me jes to cum in an thro myself on de
ignoance uv de cote."

Among the quaint characters of Biloxi is
George Ohr, the potter.   He says that he is
full of philosophy, and can argue human
nature with you all day.   His mustache is two
feet long from tip to tip, and he wears it drawn
behind his ears.   George is never tired of im-
pressing his visitors with the fact that the
fools are not all dead yet, nor all born yet.

In the rectory yard of Biloxi, a giant live

of the Southern Gulf Coast.

oak stands in the majestic beauty of its old age. In the long ago, its young branches twined a circlet that blessed two happy hearts; a circlet that is still distinctly visible, and tells to each passer-by its strange, sweet story of Indian romance.

A Biloxi chief discovered that his daughter loved the son of another chief—his bitterest enemy. When the young people pleaded their love, he turned from them with flashing eyes, and pointing wrathfully to the young oak above, exclaimed:

"No! The young fawn can never be the light of your wigwam until a ring grows in the branches of yonder oak."

And then—O, wonder of wonders!—during the succeeding night, a terrific storm twisted the young branch into a distinct ring, that grew as firm as the tree itself. The terrified old chief felt that nature commanded a blessing that he dared not refuse. For what could have worked such a marvel but the touch of the dreaded Thunder Being?

"In Sunny Mississippi," Julian Ralph tells us of the sensuous, dreamy, delicious, soothing nature of the sea-coast fever, and that no one who has it would be cured of it on any account; that a patient with it will be observed to talk rationally and to sustain ordinary light conversation, but will on no account move from a chair, unless it is to drop into the next vacant seat. He tells of the northern editor to whom was handed a New Orleans paper containing the account of the burning of his business house · but the editor pushed it away, saying :

"Let her burn. I am here for rest, and don't want business mixed up with it."

In the early days of the colony, domestic ties and happiness were left in the homes beyond the sea, and the prattle of little children was unknown in the rude cabin of the pioneer. In the love of beautiful Indian girls, there was the fascination of unlicensed freedom and a demoralization of the finer instincts. When refined, cultivated women and civilization came, as they always do, hand in hand, many of the bronzed, rugged men welcomed them eagerly, but with others an effort was required to wake them from the moral torpor into which they had fallen.

Premiums were offered to the men who would marry, and premiums were given for children. In the French and Canadian colonies, men were offered a year's pay and their discharge from the army if they would marry.

But now the coast resounds with the voices of
happy children ; their white, dimpled fingers
smooth away the cares of maturer years, and
the soft, bracing air cures all childish ailments.
It is the children's paradise of birds and flowers and dancing waters. The small army of
invaders march into the sea and embrace it,
for they love it.

There is a saying that the sea has no
friends, and that its salt waters are made of
women's tears. They tell us that when its
charms tempt the mariners far out upon its
surface, its treacherous smiles are often
changed to tempests, and they are drawn
beneath the raging waters, or the Lorelei
charms them upon the rocks of destruction.

They tell us, too, of an island, fair and
beautiful, that stood out in the sea, a seeming
haven of rest for the weary man of business,
or a flower-strewn pathway for the child of
fashion and frivolity. There a Lethean for-
getfulness of care and the distant, noisy world
wrapt them in delightful content, and little
recked they when, as the evening shadows
fell, a cloud no larger than a man's hand ap-
peared in the distant blue sky. And when the
gentle evening breeze stiffened into a gale,
and the waves broke with a dull boom upon

the shore, it was to the revelers only the ex-
hilaration of a beautiful danger far removed.
The ball-room's mingled sounds vied with the
tempest's noise without;—the sounds of
mingled music and laughter, the gentle murmur of friendship, or the impetuous words
that woke with the dawn of love. But the
sea, envious of this joyous scene, dashed its
strong waves against the building, and shook
it with fearful power. The cruel waters
suddenly crept over the ball-room floor,
over the satin slippers and dancing feet;
trembling words were stayed upon pallid lips;
the wild instinct of flight was met with a
fiercer invasion of the waters, and the swaying, fainting figures were engulfed in seething
waves.

The morning dawned upon a sea that was
calm and beautiful, but it held within its
sepulchral depths over a hundred lifeless forms
that only a few hours before had been instinct
with happiness and hope. A Lost Island had
sunk far beneath its depths, and ever afterward was only a memory of tragic horror.

The sea, however, is always beautiful—
beautiful beyond description when the sublime
tempest seems to mingle sea and sky in a
scene of tumultuous ruin, and beautiful beyond

words, when in the enchanting calm of a summer morning, it breaks upon the shining sands
of the shore "with a lace-like frill of foamy
ripples and wavelets."

Not alone do the voices of children and
beautiful homes contrast the past with the
present, but commerce and trade are opening
every avenue of business and speak of the
progress of the Nineteenth Century.

The time has passed when the Indian
roamed these shores with passive possession,
and thought that a gunshot was a brave, but
a letter was a fraud. The white man's speaking bark speeds from the morning's press to
every point of the compass. The realized
prophecy that thought shall fly around the
world in the twinkling of an eye is not more
wonderful than the progress of steam, and the
electric illumination that reveals to us the
hidden secrets of science. Man, the inventor
and discoverer, pauses with astonishment at
the wonders of his creation, and often some
modern convenience of every-day life starts a
train of thought, boundless in its possibilities.
Back in the thirties many of these things
would only have been considered wild flights
of imagination, for as late as 1839, there were
no telegraphs nor railroads in Mississippi.

In the early settlement of the sea-coast, the vision of expectancy went no further than buffalo wool and pearl fisheries, and gems that would rival those of Peru and Mexico. The colonists starved in the midst of unknown riches. Crozat lost millions there, the India Company lost over twenty millions and the king over fifty millions.

But now the country blooms like a garden. The Alsatians and Germans, the first gardeners who were tempted here by John Laws' brilliant bubble, little dreamed of the vast possibility of the trade which they commenced. Vegetables of every variety are raised; also figs, pears, peaches, plums, pomegranates, pecan nuts, persimmons, oranges, etc. The Concord, Scuppernong Delaware and Ives Seedling give to the coast magnificent vineyards, and the industries of wine making, agriculture, and dairying flourish; sheep and hogs also thrive.

Immense quantities of the rarest and richest fruits and vegetables are shipped from the coast. The breath of the tropics is wafted to the frozen North to tell them that summer lives to come to them again, and that it always gladdens this beautiful sea-shore of the sunny South. Mississippi's forest territory is more than twenty-one millions of acres. The rapid development of the state can be partially appreciated from the fact that in 1880 capital invested in manufacturing was $257,244,000, and in 1894 it was $800,000,000; the value of manufactured products in 1880 was $457,454,-777, and in 1894 it was $1,000,000,000.

On the sea-coast, vessels from all parts of the earth wait to be laden with lumber from the great southern pine belt—Moss Point alone having a sawmill worth a quarter of million dollars. King Cotton's fleecy staple is shipped; all the products of agriculture and manufacture, and the great product of Louisiana, the vast Sugar Bowl of America. And the world is happier that there is such a Southland to send forth her treasures.

All along the sea-shore stand the immense live oaks, like giant sentinels bringing past and present together, and from their branches swings the beautiful Spanish moss.

"As by some fairy fingers spun
        It trembles to the wind's soft sigh,
    It sways to kisses of the sun
        As cloud-wreaths mingle in the sky.
    The wild bird gathers for her brood
        The floss to line her sylvan nest,
    It screens her tender solitude
        And softly veils her bed of rest."

It was on the southern sea-shore that the genius of Audubon, the great Louisiana naturalist, first awoke. The brilliant plumage of Louisiana birds won his boyish admiration, and afterward became themes of scientific study that made his name world-wide.

Here are found all varieties of birds that are a source of delight to the man of science, or to the reckless sportsman. Nor does the destructive touch of the latter spare the snipe, so sacred to the Biloxian, because that bird was the sister of the Thunder Being.

Along the coast are vast canneries, that ship vegetables, fruit and fish, and the diamond-back terrapin farms equal the famous ones of Maryland. There are woolen and cotton factories, and the rod and reel are a source of pleasure and profit. Here are found black bass, pompano, sheepshead, redfish, and too many others to mention. Their marvelous and resplendent coloring lifts the heart involuntarily to the Creator of this beautiful world. To us are given the treasures of earth, sea and sky.

Yellow fever, a visitor so much dreaded in the past, is gradually but surely being conquered by improved and scientific knowledge of the disease. For eighteen years it did not

lift its saffron head, but when in 1897 its waves
of terror swept over the South, the disease, by
contrast with the past, proved to be a terror in
name only.

On the sea-coast the fainting heart of the
invalid is revived, his pale cheeks are bronzed
by aquatic sports, and the blood flows stronger
through his weakened body. He sleeps while
the mocking-bird fills the night air with trills
of purest melody, and, dreaming of heavenly
rest, he forgets the pain and weariness of living.

The wide halls sweep from end to end
of airy houses, and the verandas encircling
shadows tempt one to constant enjoyment of
fresh-air treatment.

When frost lays its lace-like net-work on
the windows of northern homes, here they
are opened wide for the warm, sweet air
that is perfumed by the jasmine, the magnolia
and the orange flowers, and roses climbing to
the tops of trellises mingle their rainbow hues
of beauty. With it all, like a refrain of
soft, rippling music, there is that strange, inexplicable, but restful influence of the sea:

> "Ah! what pleasant visions haunt me
> As I gaze upon the sea!
> All the old romantic legends,
> All my dreams, come back to me.

of the Southern Gulf Coast.

Sails of silk, and ropes of sandal,
 Such as gleam in ancient lore;
And the singing of the sailors,
 And the answer from the shore!

Till my soul is full of longing
 For the secret of the sea,
And the heart of the great ocean
 Sends a thrilling pulse through me."

www.ingramcontent.com/pod-product-compliance
Lightning Source LLC
Chambersburg PA
CBHW030602270326
41927CB00007B/1013